the PR

BUZZ
factor

the PR BUZZ factor

how using public relations can boost your business

russell lawson

Foreword by Carol Undy, Chair of the Federation of Small Businesses

KOGAN
PAGE

London and Philadelphia

First published in Great Britain and the United States in 2006 by Kogan Page Limited

120 Pentonville Road
London N1 9JN
United Kingdom
www.kogan-page.co.uk

525 South 4th Street, #241
Philadelphia PA 19147
USA

© Russell Lawson, 2006

The right of Russell Lawson to be identified as the author of this work has been asserted by him in accordance with the Copyright, Designs and Patents Act 1988.

ISBN 0 7494 4468 1

British Library Cataloguing-in-Publication Data

A CIP record for this book is available from the British Library.

Library of Congress Cataloging-in-Publication Data

Lawson, Russell.
    The PR buzz factor : how using public relations can boost your business.
        p. cm.
    Includes index.
    ISBN 0-7494-4468-1
    1. Public relations. 2. Strategic planning. I. Title.
HD59.L42 2006
659.2—dc22

                                        2005035382

Typeset by Saxon Graphics Ltd, Derby
Printed and bound in the United States by Thomson-Shore, Inc

Contents

Foreword

Carol Undy

Chair, Federation of Small Businesses

What is the true purpose of public relations and how can it really help impact the growth of your small business?

In order for the media to succeed, they need information that is both useful and entertaining for their readers. This is where you, the business owner, come in.

Anyone who's cynical towards the importance of learning new skills has never owned a small business. I own one and know that, at times when deadlines, suppliers, customers and staff are piling pressure on, recalling words of wisdom simply lifts me out of a slump.

Success leaves clues: successful people leave clues on how to win. eBay's founders boasted that they spent no money on advertising apart from PR for two years. That's a big clue for anyone in business.

When thinking of public relations, many things may come to mind, like: sweaty palms as you pick up the phone to try to convince a reporter how great your business is; getting writer's block while trying to write a press release about your company; or countless hours of faxing your story to hundreds of editors just to find out that your piece did not make it to print.

However, public relations does not have to be such a daunting effort. If done right, public relations can also bring rewarding thoughts to your mind, like: the constant ringing of phones in your office of people interested in your products or services; gaining credibility and becoming a leading expert in your industry; or thousands of people learning about your company in a matter of days without costing you a penny!

Most small business owners think that public relations is too time-consuming an effort. This may be true in cases where small businesses have very limited resources, but this should not discourage you from doing it. It is just a matter of prioritizing your goals and using the resources that you do have available to take advantage of what is an invaluable marketing tactic.

A company that is 'in the news' is more visible and more interesting. Good publicity can attract capital, partners and employees as well as potential customers. It can position a business as 'the expert', 'thought leader' and 'go-to people'.

The publicity generated is almost always the most valuable and cost-effective way of promoting an offering. Unlike an advertisement, editorial publicity carries the perception of an unbiased third-party endorsement. And the benefits of a positive endorsement by the media can hardly be overstated.

What is required from you is to keep in your mind your vision of the perfect PR-knowing small business you want to become. Nothing is more important to the development of a business career, or any endeavour, than the dream it's seeking to fulfil.

As Lowell Paxson said: 'Effective leaders are visionaries. They see something out there in the distance that others don't yet see. They're convinced that the ordinary can be transformed into something successful. Leaders have a vivid imagination, and they're persuaded that what is only a distant dream today will be a reality tomorrow.'

Introduction:
What makes you tick?

This brief introduction covers the factors that make a small business tick – why you are different from large businesses, what is important to you, and why taking a 'step back' from the business and looking at its growth strategically is so important to small business success.

Business is a war...

Business is a war where the big business managers are the NCOs who lead according to a well laid down discipline, and the self-employed are the independent marauders who identify opportunities to murder, rape and pillage, paying scant attention to the formal rules of warfare. In the war of survival, small businesses are natural casualties. The miracle is that there are so many of them that actually survive.

Jim Torrance, Federation of Small Businesses

But small business is big business: it is an army of around 4 million small firms that account for more than half of the private workforce in the country and more than half of all sales.

If you have picked up this book because you fall into this category, then congratulations – you are part of an army that has 12 million people working for it and is joined by another half a million new recruits every year. You are critical to the economy of the country. This is not simply a political catchphrase or sound bite: you offer services at local levels that large businesses do not.

In addition, you are the 'seedbed of innovation', stimulating competition. Over 60 per cent of all commercial innovations come from small firms.

You also mop up jobs lost in large companies. Strategies to encourage start-ups and promote small business growth have been successfully implemented both in Los Angeles, California and in the East Midlands region of England following the closure of large textile companies.

And you are the large firms of tomorrow. Marks and Spencer, Rolls-Royce and Boots are all small-business success stories, as is Virgin, which was started by four people in a church crypt in the late 1960s.

Your business is the realization of a dream and the belief that you personally can succeed without the protection of a corporation. You are your own boss, and nobody can take that away from you.

But all is not rosy for you. It's hard to be an owner-manager: running the business, finding the markets, coping with regulations, finding the staff, looking for finance, dealing with problems. The pace of change is ever increasing and you have to respond to it. Long-term planning is becoming more and more difficult.

You now have many competing pressures on you and find yourself living with smaller margins and tighter cash flow. Costs are increasing but have to be absorbed. Global markets and global competitors mean that you need to move even faster…

What makes you tick?

Sooner or later in everyone's working life, the question arises, 'If I'm so good at what I do and produce good business and profits for my employer, why can't I do this for myself?'

Then it becomes a question of confidence and – to a great degree – courage in taking your financial resources and laying them on the line, knowing that there is always the seed of doubt, 'What if I get it wrong?' But countering this, there is always the hope that you can create something that, if it is successful, can afford a better lifestyle for yourself and your family.

A small business is usually run by a few people who have to take on a number of roles, who often have a personal financial commitment in the business and whose success depend on results, not just the time that is spent in work.

The personal bond between the owners and staff must be essentially a strong one. Without sounding trite, it must encompass mutual respect and the realization that everyone is working towards a common goal.

There are no numbers in small businesses – names and individuals are what it is all about. And there is no room for the blinkered attitude found in large firms of 'it's not my job'.

In a small firm, staff must be flexible in their working arrangements and have a belief in the business, which cannot just be looked at as a 'job'. There must be good relationships between the owner and staff, and working as a team is essential to achieve these objectives. All members of staff must be ready to take on responsibilities outside their usual functions.

And people who run small firms need to be multi-talented, flexible and very hard working. Staff loyalty is vital in small business. Customers expect a better and more personal service than they do from large organizations. Courtesy and a willingness to work are essential at all levels.

A small business owner must always be alert to market changes and be planning well ahead. Too much reliance on one large company to provide work can be very dangerous. Small businesses can adapt more quickly to the market as decision making is not burdened by the hierarchy of a large business – this is particularly true in the leisure and tourism marketplace.

A small business has to value every customer. A large firm can afford to simply choose not to deal with certain customers. Conversely, a small number of payment defaulters can much more seriously affect a small business, so care is required in that direction. The small business has to be constantly aware of market trends and anticipate demand, whereas to a large extent big firms can create demand.

The importance of the owner is paramount. The workforce must have confidence in his or her business skills and ability to render decisions for the continued well-being of the firm. However, sometimes difficult or unpopular decisions have to be made – it goes with the territory. Honesty with oneself, the workforce and clients is of ultimate importance, as is a well-developed sense of overall justice and an ability to laugh at oneself and be humble enough to admit mistakes.

If the owner does not make the business tick, then it will fail. The owner must know the market inside out and has to be a 'jack of all trades'. The owner must have the ability to carry out an ongoing assessment that what the business is offering is what the market wants. Having the flexibility to change quickly, monitoring customer reaction, taking advice as required and keeping tight financial control are also crucial elements.

The owner's contribution and participation are vital to success. In the absence of a full, professional management team, the owner is required to take all-important decisions and is relied on to maintain morale. People-management skills are very important unless the business either involves very few participants or has a large staff turnover, and obviously the latter is undesirable.

Networking is very important, and good relations with other small firms are essential, which non-business parts of a local community sometimes misinterpret. It is important that the business puts over to the community as a whole the benefits that come with a vibrant small-business sector. Small businesses must be an integral part of the community and cannot remain aloof, as can large businesses. But this does in turn create additional pressures.

Small is beautiful, and the decisions small firms make are based on personal experience, access to market research, and advice from professional advisers. They have the flexibility to change tack to meet changing or new market needs quickly. The decisions they make in the next 12 months will directly have a bearing on their profitability and will ultimately determine their ability to continue to trade. What better incentive do they need to get it right?

They have the advantage of freedom over large firms because they have no management team, board of directors or shareholders to answer to. They can make instant decisions and these are final. That is not to say that every decision they make is the correct one, but there is much advantage in being able to make a major decision without having to spend time consulting with others. Basically, if they spot a trend, they can respond instantly.

In contrast, big business employs people to carry out specific tasks and there is often little incentive to put in more than is required within a set working pattern or to carry out functions for which they are not paid. But one big problem in a small business – and this is the gap this handbook will fill – is that professional advice or particular expertise is not often available in-house and has to be brought in as required. A small business uses all of the management skills required by big business. However, it does not have the luxury of appointing a specialist for each task.

A small business, by virtue of the fact that it is small, does not usually have a large marketing budget so it is essential that the owner is highly astute and precise in identifying potential markets. Large business is more concerned with corporate image, while a small firm is concerned with the image that the individual and the workforce present, as well as the products it offers.

What is public relations?

Public relations (hereafter known as 'PR') is probably the most widely misunderstood side of marketing. It suffers from the image of being a gaggle of spin doctors who gloss over badly run corporate or public sector schemes. Not many people would argue against the need to promote their business in a positive light, but at the same time they look upon PR as a luxury that is not absolutely necessary and costs too much money, which is why only large firms do it. In fact, for small businesses PR can be something very different.

Small businesses are actually at a big advantage when it comes to PR. It gives them the ability to project themselves as big, multibillion-pound businesses, all for the cost of some well-strategized PR plans. Quite simply, PR campaigns for small businesses have the ability to reach into untapped markets and in the long haul small businesses are able to build a brand for themselves and their products.

So what does a successful PR programme mean for a small business? At the end of it you will have achieved three major things:

1. You will be able to demonstrate your expertise in your sector of the market.
2. You will have established credibility for your company and products.
3. You will have created loyalty among your buyers and attracted potential customers.

These are priceless assets that many big companies would kill for (as the expression goes). They spend millions trying to associate the first two of these properties with their company's image by means of their name, their logo, their advertising jingles, etc. They want to be seen as 'the authority' in their field and they know that these two attributes can lead to that perception.

They spend millions more trying to achieve the third item in the list by 'good citizen' ploys like Ronald McDonald, supporting good causes through sponsorships, etc. They desperately want to be seen as 'caring corporate citizens' because that leads to the most elusive and valuable asset of all: customer loyalty. Yet rarely, if ever, do they achieve complete success.

This is because their size works against them. People don't credit a company with expertise if their dealings are always with the lowest and most inexperienced minions. They don't consider hollow-sounding canned responses by customer service staff – which are meant to project a caring attitude – to be credible. As for winning customer loyalty, the more attempts that large corporations make to win repeat business from customers, the more cynical people become. Contrary to most areas where small businesses compete with their larger cousins, this is one that small businesses should find easy and win every time. The irony is that *they hardly ever try*.

I know what you're thinking – all this sounds very good but, let's face it, small businesses can have a much tougher time if they try to approach the press the same way big organizations do. The overall media industry (newspapers, magazines, TV, radio and online journals) mindset is that big business is news and small business is, well, rarely news.

You have to keep in mind that the current big conglomerates used to be small businesses as well, like McDonald's, which started off as one local restaurant in California. So what did they have? What was that something extra that allowed them to grow into giants? Of course, it would be an exaggeration to say that an understanding of the importance of PR is all that singled them out, but, make no mistake, it was a major factor in their growth!

But as we shall go on to discover, good PR for a small business can be your most effective promotional activity, while also being the least expensive.

About this book

This book will address this sticky issue of making PR relevant to *your* business. It is a simple-to-use tool that you will use to judge your current reputation and help you step by step to devise a strategy to send out the messages you need to your own diverse audiences (your customers, your suppliers, your staff, etc); differentiate you from your competition; and position you as an authoritative industry voice within your sector.

This is very much a 'hands-on' book, which is written in a practical, interactive way by giving you the necessary tools to analyse your own business in PR terms in order to reach your relevant target audience, gain wide distribution and exposure within these audiences, and communicate your key messages.

The difference between this book and many other 'business help books' you may have picked up is that this will be relevant to *you* and *your individual business*. It is relevant not only to you as an owner-manager, but also in the industry in which you work.

It will help you develop a range of strategic skills so that you can plan your business. It will not only make the subject of PR relevant to the daily activities of your business, but will, at the same time, give you a strategic overview of how your business can be more successful.

It's no coincidence that a large survey of entrepreneurs told the Council for Excellence in Management and Leadership (CEML) that the crucial qualities for success were strategic and analytical thinking abilities. These included, for example, setting a vision, strategy and goals for the business, as well as having skills for clear communication.

Although at first glance you might think that this book looks a bit complicated, in fact what it is doing is almost alarmingly simple! In essence, it is helping *you* to take a structured approach to putting *your* business in a good light by:

- looking at where you are starting from in terms of reputation within your business sector and then establishing the audiences you need to reach;
- considering the messages that you need to send them, *how* you want them to respond and *when* you need them to react;
- then selecting the channels through which to communicate to them, looking at costs, how to manage the channels and how to sustain them.

There, that's actually quite straightforward, isn't it? But done right, this simple formula can be the most effective way of increasing profits that you could possibly imagine!

What's in this book?

- *Chapter 1: Audit – where are you now?* The initial part of the diagnostic tool is used here. Firstly, you fill in a simple questionnaire for your own use. Then another simple questionnaire is outlined to enable you to approach your suppliers, employees and clients in order to determine the perceptions of the effectiveness of your business. With this information, you can answer a series of straightforward questions regarding your business, its sector, its background and its requirements.

- *Chapter 2: Why you need PR.* This chapter shows why PR is so important to small-business success. Contrary to most areas where small businesses compete with their larger cousins, this is one that small businesses should find easy and win every time. The chapter will clearly demonstrate that good PR, for a small business, can be the most effective promotional activity you can undertake, while at the same time being the least expensive!

- *Chapter 3: Environmental analysis.* Here we guide you through conducting a PEST (political, environmental, social, technological) and a SWOT (strengths, weaknesses, opportunities, threats) analysis by suggesting as many areas for finding information as possible. The difference with this analysis, however, is that when looking at opportunities it will take into account points identified in the PEST analysis. This means that opportunities will be identified that can be taken advantage of in your business's current working environment. You will be able to draw up tangible PR objectives, which will be central to your current business goals and objectives.

- *Chapter 4: Your communication strategy.* This is where we look at how your business is going to identify the people who are going to help it realize these new PR goals. We look at their expectations and shows how to identify which ones carry the most power and interest in what your business is trying to achieve. We look at what messages need to be sent to these key people, suggest channels for these messages and give ideas on cost, also suggesting ways these should be monitored to gauge the achievement of your objectives. Imaginative ways to record how you are presented in the media are also outlined. The use of the internet is shown as a key tool in the PR battle, and suggestions for its design are given.

- *Chapter 5: Implementing your plan.* This is where the tactics of the strategy come into play. We throw all sorts of suggestions at you that you can easily implement as part of a successful PR campaign, such as developing research surveys, negotiating in-magazine surveys to be run in conjunction with leading publications, forming strategic alliances with appropriate partners to enforce the credibility and authority of a brand, increasing press coverage by drawing up media coverage targets, creating a virtual press office, creating newsletters, getting celebrity endorsement, etc.

- *Chapter 6: Keeping it going.* This is a summary chapter encouraging you to stick with your PR campaign, which also opens up new avenues for your PR activities, such as guidelines for selecting and briefing a media evaluation company and what to look for when working with a PR agency.

1 The audit

Introduction

Here is where we really start getting down to business. As with all great journeys, before looking at where we want to go we need to find out where we are now. In this chapter a simple diagnostic tool will be used: the keys points that you know and perceive about your business will be written down and then a simple two-page questionnaire will be filled in for future use. Another simple questionnaire will be outlined to enable you to approach your suppliers, employees and clients in order to determine the perceptions of the effectiveness of your business. With this information, you can then answer a series of straightforward questions regarding your business's sector, organization, background and PR requirements. Finally, we will look at the whole area of strategy and tactics, and decide which tactics are the ones best suited to your current situation.

First, a bit about you...

This handbook has been written with you in mind. How do I know who you are? I've worked with many people like you, and I've spoken to people like you about what you want out of books like this. These are the things that you have told me:

- Although you are largely confident in your day-to-day management capabilities, you are not satisfied with the managerial abilities in a strategic sense, ie the ability to see the 'big picture' for your business.
- Although you see an inherent value in being able to put together a strategic PR campaign, and the benefits this could bring to your firm, you find it difficult to identify your own personal 'knowledge' needs in this area and how these can best be met.
- You don't have the time to spend learning a new discipline, although you are aware that your larger competitors are more successful because they can afford to have their middle managers take time out of the business in order to attend courses.
- PR is not related to the business world; therefore it is of very little value (although I hope you've changed your view by now).
- It is hard to get PR to be relevant to your business: it needs to be relevant not only to you, but also to the industry in which you work.
- You demand new methods of learning that are compact, easy to understand through use of diagrams and examples, and not unduly onerous. Offerings to small businesses are usually too big and complex, and there needs to be an initial step of demonstrating the benefits of learning so you can judge whether the whole thing is worth it.
- You believe that learning needs to be relevant to the daily activities of your business but at the same time give a strategic overview of how your firm could be more successful.

The big challenges

The two big challenges facing us now are: 1) to make a PR strategy relevant to your own business; and 2) to make it fairly simple to undertake (you haven't got the time to learn rocket science).

This handbook now turns its attention to showing you a hands-on way of helping you to put together some PR objectives and ways to achieve them; to helping you to examine your own business so you can fit your PR objectives in with your overall business direction; to showing you how to use various techniques to meet your new PR (and business) objectives; and, finally, to showing you how to monitor your plan in order to make sure it runs smoothly and then to evaluate how successful it has been.

This is, in a nutshell, what you will have got out of this book: and what you get out of anything depends on what you put in! I'm afraid, like most things, you'll need to put a bit of effort in over the following pages, but the more effort you put in then the more rewards you will reap at the end of it.

Over the following chapters we will be taking part in a carefully laid-out plan. We will conduct a context analysis where we will analyse the situation that your firm is in and the factors that affect it by looking at the political, economic, social and technological pulls on it. Then we will examine the strengths, weaknesses, opportunities and threats associated with your own business.

We will then analyse the outside factors that are affecting your firm, and identify opportunities: things that you can actually take advantage of. Then we can determine your business's strengths and weaknesses, and identify fundamental and marginal strengths and weaknesses. This means that we can then relate your business's fundamental strengths to outside opportunities. The idea is that we have found opportunities that we can match to your company's main strengths, giving you some dead-cert winning areas to focus on!

This information then allows us to frame objectives for your company, let's say three objectives, that would be specific, measurable, achievable, relevant and have deadlines.

We would then fit in these objectives with those of the company (if you have any – don't worry if you haven't: we'll cover this too), such as your:

- organizational goals;
- business objectives;
- marketing/sales objectives;
- service-delivery or brand/product objectives;
- communications objectives.

Then it's time for the PR strategy. This is where we look at the people who are going to help us realize your goals, ie your stakeholders. The sorts of groups we are talking about are:

- the community at large or people living near or affected by your business's premises or practices;
- employees, managers and their unions;
- customers – past, present and future;
- suppliers of materials and non-financial services;
- the money market, including shareholders, banks, insurers and investors;
- distributors, agents, wholesalers and retailers;
- potential employees, consultants and agents;
- opinion leaders, particularly radio, television, press and other media professionals or activists, including lobbyists and pressure groups.

Then we look at the expectations of these stakeholders and identify which ones carry the most power and interest in what we are trying to achieve. We will develop a campaign to reposition certain stakeholders and to identify who are the key blockers of change and how we can respond to them in terms of education. We also have to maintain levels of interest among key players in order to ensure a successful PR campaign.

We will do this by examining the messages we need to send each of our key audiences, and look at channels for delivery and how to cost them. In addition, we will see ways these can be monitored to gauge the achievement of our objectives, such as involvement and observation, regular reporting, questioning and discussion, and records and routine statistics, with an idea of how much money this will cost.

I will guarantee that if you go through this process wholeheartedly then you will not only have a good PR campaign leading to increased profits but you will also have a better idea of how you can improve your overall business!

So you should now have a good idea of where we are going. However, before setting any objectives about where your business wants to be in terms of its 'public image', we have to look at where it is now. Before you can determine future strategy you have to know where you are!

Case study

Background

Friends Reunited – www.friendsreunited.co.uk – is a website that puts old school and college friends back in touch with each other. It was set up by Barnet couple Steve and Julie Pankhurst in October 2000. Beatwax Communications was employed in April 2001 when the site had 30,000 registered users.

Objectives

- To raise the profile of the site to the British adult population.
- To encourage registration.
- Issues management.

Execution and implementation

Beatwax initially worked with the *Guardian*'s G2 on a feature positioning Friends Reunited as the 'next big thing'. This was followed one week later with features placed in *The Times* and the *Evening Standard*. This ignited broadcast interest and the creators appeared on *London Tonight* and the 6 pm *BBC News*. They also conducted various radio interviews.

Beatwax Communications was conscious of the backlash against the dotcom industry and therefore positioned Friends Reunited as a family website operated from a back bedroom in Barnet. It nurtured the idea of Julie working on the site from a laptop balanced on her knee while looking after her daughter and watching *EastEnders*. The media subsequently warmed to this internet venture.

A number of heart-warming case studies were sourced through the site and fed to the tabloids for human interest features. The *Sun* was contacted initially for mass market support. To maximize the number of national papers covering the story, Beatwax researched different angles.

E-mails regarding the site were sent to a diverse range of contacts in order to capitalize on the inherent curiosity of journalists to rediscover their past. Beatwax paid particular attention to publicizing the site via TV as this proved to be the most effective way of driving traffic to the site and increasing registrations. They contacted the major magazine and news programmes with a case study or a view to Steve and Julie appearing.

Regional media were offered local angles where users had successfully been reunited. The Press Association was frequently updated with site statistics, which in turn generated further regional coverage. The site was pitched to online and trade journalists as the potential internet success story of the year.

As the site became more popular, the PR consultants began to source features for Steve and Julie, perpetuating the site's family image. Certain issues arising from the site required careful media management. Beatwax always tried to ensure a positive outcome.

The campaign was not backed up by any advertising.

Measurement and evaluation

Every national newspaper has featured the site on more than one occasion. The number of registered users was 30,000 in April 2001 when Beatwax commenced work on the account. By February 2002, the site had over 5 million registered users.

In April 2001 the site had 1.5 million hits per month. In February 2002 the site peaked at 9 million hits in one day! The site was in the top 10 most visited websites in the UK in 2001, an achievement shared with the likes of MSN, Freeserve and the BBC.

Through its period of exceptional growth (September–November 2001), Friends Reunited was the most searched-for site on www.msn.co.uk. Friends Reunited appeared as a successful brand awareness campaign in *PR Week*, 6 October 2001.

Creativity

Beatwax encouraged journalists to register on the site and actively organize a reunion. They offered free upgrades to enable this. They created a rapport with the users of the site, capitalizing on positive eventualities like people getting married as a result of meeting through the site.

Beatwax encouraged celebrities and broadcasters to log on to the site and look at their old school friends. For instance, the *Daily Mail* featured a double-page spread on celebrities and their old school friends, and radio host Chris Moyles discussed the site at length on Radio 1. A weekly feature was negotiated with the *Sunday Express*, offering human interest stories and topical case studies, for instance Valentine's Day. This commenced in January 2002.

As the Friends Reunited database expanded into the millions, Beatwax contacted TV researchers offering it as a resource in return for positive on-air recognition for the site. The site kick-started the nostalgia phenomenon across Britain, and Beatwax recognized an opportunity to extend the Friends Reunited concept to TV.

Beatwax approached *Revolution*, a key internet trade magazine, to feature a monthly diary column written by co-founder Steve Pankhurst. This commenced in January 2002.

Friends Reunited has become a household name, aided by the great concept and viral nature of the product and superb PR – there can be few who have not read about, or been touched by, the site over the past year.

The company has successfully ditched the dotcom tag and demonstrated through clever media relations how the internet offers a unique way to reach people and, in many cases, instigate friendships and reunions. The response to this from the media was truly phenomenal and this translated directly into a massive increase in registered users

The audit

The dreaded audit! Yes, I'm afraid in the world of PR there is a need for a stocktake! It's essential, as a marketing audit allows you to see the big picture – the true picture.

Only if you study the past can you foretell the future! It will help you to understand why customers want, or do not want, your products or services, the motives underlying their purchases, what is affecting their behaviour, why and how customers buy and who influences their buying decisions.

Have you ever sat down and described your company and the industry it operates in, using both positive and negative perceptions and facts? What is the nature of your business? Where is it located? What is the size, market share, turnover, etc? And what is the overall business opportunity or problem?

What is your product or service? What is it called? What does it do? How does it work? What percentage is it of the market and what is your market share? What competitors does it have? What are the unique selling points? What are the distinguishing features of each product? Can you translate the features into benefits?

How about your customers? At all times, in your business cycle, you have three main target market groups: your present or existing customers – active and inactive; your past customers; and your prospective or new customers. They are the most important ingredients in your PR strategy. As Anita Roddick of The Body Shop says: 'Don't sell to everybody; sell to somebody!'

What was the market opportunity that brought your product into existence? Has the original opportunity changed? If so, why? What external, unforeseen circumstances enhanced or retarded your marketing, campaigns, strategy and plans? What are the number of years and money spent on previous marketing strategies? Have you ever done any research on the success or failure of your current strategy? Is the research valid?

Does your creative approach to your business fit with your products, target market and corporate identity? What are your short- and long-term marketing objectives, and with what yardstick will you measure success or failure? What do you want your present, past and potential customer to do? What is your 'offer' strategy?

What other marketing or advertising is planned? What are your primary and secondary merchandising objectives? What are your distribution objectives? What is the distribution pattern and how is it done and by whom, and what percentage of the costs or price is it? Is it effective and cost-effective?

Loyal employees create loyal customers. Employee loyalty increases business profitability, competitiveness and market share. What, how, when, where, why and to whom do you communicate? And how does it fit in with your overall plans?

Which industries, companies or products can be tied in with your products? Looking at your products and services now and the objectives to be met, do you know enough about the market, the target market and the competition? What existing research is available? What further research should be undertaken to help you plan your PR and marketing strategy?

Who, what, why, when, where and how? It's not easy doing an intangible audit. If you sell tables, you count how many you've made, how many you've sold and how many are left in the storeroom. Although not always easy, it's still pretty straightforward. But when doing an audit of concepts like 'Why do I have the customers I have and why don't I have more?', things get a bit more tricky.

You could literally spend days if not weeks undertaking the kind of audit outlined above. Instead, what we need to do is build a simple profile of your business. What you need to do is circle the words below that apply to you. This is not an exact science, so circle the ones that apply the most to how you feel – but you must be brutal! You need to be as honest as you possibly can to build up an accurate picture. After all, you'll be the only one looking at this anyway.

Your sector

Profile of market or sector: size, dynamics, trends
Circle the words in bold that apply to you:

Is your market **big, medium-sized** or **small**?
Is it a **fast-changing** or **slow-changing** market?
Is it a **growing** or **static** market?

Your organization's status and reputation
Circle the words in bold that apply to you:

Would you say your customers were **loyal** or **opportunist**?
Would you say your suppliers were **loyal** or **opportunist**?
Would you say your customers and suppliers saw you as a **big** or a **small** company?

Competitors' status and reputation; role models
Circle the words in bold that apply to you:

Would you say your competitors' customers were **loyal** or **opportunist**?
Would you say your competitors' suppliers were **loyal** or **opportunist**?
Would you say your competitors were **big** or **small** companies?

Profile of customers/stakeholders in market or sector
Circle the words in bold that apply to you:

Would you say that, in the main, your customers were **old, young, middle-aged** or a **balance** of all three?
Are they mostly **male, female** or a **balance**?
Would you say they were **rich, poor** or **reasonably well off**? (Use your own judgement here.)

Characteristics – seasonal/regional
Circle the words in bold that apply to you:

Are your customers mostly **local, regional** or **national**?
Do you sell more in the **spring, summer, autumn** or **winter**, or is it steady **year-round**?

Your organization

Description of your business – what does it actually do?
Circle the words in bold that apply to you:

Do you provide a **product** or a **service**?
If a product, do you **manufacture, wholesale** or **retail**? If a service, do you **provide directly** or **subcontract**?

Background and history
Circle the words in bold that apply to you:

Is your business **under 5** years old, **between 5 and 10** years old or **over 10** years old?
Are you the **founder** of the business or the **successor** in it?

Mission and values
Circle the words in bold that apply to you:

I have or **I have not** got a mission statement.
I have or **I have not** got the values of my business written down.

Objectives and goals
Circle the words in bold that apply to you:

I have or **I have not** got business objectives that are written down.
I have or **I have not** got marketing and sales objectives that are written down.
I have or **I have not** got product-/service-specific objectives.

Unique selling points
Circle the words in bold that apply to you:

Are you **acutely aware**, **quite aware** or **vaguely aware** of your product's or service's unique selling point(s)?
Do you see the unique selling point(s) of your product or service as **vital**, **useful** or **relatively unimportant** to your business? (And remember, be honest!)

Organizational/management structure
Circle the words in bold that apply to you:

I have or **I have not** got a management structure in place.
Are there **formal** or **informal** lines of reporting in place between different employees?

Where does your business want to be in three to five years?
Circle the words in bold that apply to you:

Do you want to **grow significantly**, **grow gradually** or **not grow at all** over the next three to five years?
Do you want to be **smaller** than your main competitor, **the same size** as your main competitor or **bigger** than your main competitor in five years' time?

Are you sitting comfortably?

OK, so now we have some simple background about your business. We're starting to see what makes your business tick, and we will tell ourselves a little story about your business. Taking each of the words you circled in order, fill in the blanks in the passage in the box below.

My business operates in a market that is _____, _____ and _____. My customers are _____, my suppliers are _____ and they see me as a _____ company.

The age of my customers is mostly _____ and their gender is mostly _____. As for their pockets, they are mostly _____. They are usually from _____ areas, and they mostly come out (in the) _____.

My business provides a _____, which I _____. It is a business that is _____ years old, and I am the _____ of it.

_____ got a mission statement written down, and _____ got the values of my business written down. _____ got business objectives that are written down, _____ got marketing and sales objectives that are written down and _____ got product-/service-specific objectives.

I am _____ of my product's or service's unique selling point(s), which I regard as _____ to my business.

_____ got a management structure in place, and there are _____ lines of reporting in place between different employees. I want the business to _____ over the next three to five years and, compared to my main competitor, I want to be _____.

And there you have it! A snapshot of your business, your customers, your reputation and your aspirations. It all looks quite different written down, doesn't it? Don't underestimate how useful this exercise has been: many small businesses never get this far in taking a look at themselves!

Now we have audited what you are all about, we need to do the same kind of groundwork for our PR strategy. Continuing along the same lines, complete the following parts of the exercise.

Communication background

PR and marketing history – what worked and what did not?
Circle the words in bold that apply to you:

Do PR and marketing have a **major** or **minor** role in your business?
I have or **I have not** undertaken marketing and PR campaigns in the past.

If you have undertaken such campaigns:
Circle the words in bold that apply to you:

Were they **successful, unsuccessful** or was it **hard to tell**?
Was the person responsible for the campaign(s) **myself, an employee** or **an outside organization**?

Are you still sitting comfortably?

So to finish off your story, complete the final paragraph in the box below.

PR has a _____ role in my business. _____ undertaken marketing and PR campaigns in the past. (If you *have*, fill in the rest of this paragraph.) _____ is the way I would describe them, and _____ was the person in charge of the campaign(s).

Congratulations, you've finished the first part of your audit! A few paragraphs might not look that impressive, but if you've been completely honest in this process it will give you some very useful material to work with. However, there is still some way to go in this process, and we will continue to make some headway with the following section.

Gathering information

Performing audits is all about gathering information. Up until now you have clarified your own views and opinions on important matters, but now we will focus on gathering information that is relevant to your business. There are two basic types of information that you should start to collect: 1) literature: your own and that of your competitors; 2) market research (internal and external sources).

Literature

This is also known as 'desk research'. There are plenty of sources of information readily to hand that can provide a wealth of useful information. If appropriate, look at the annual reports, public accounting records and credit reports of your own business and those of your main competitors. How healthy do they look? Do they speak of a company moving forward, expanding and being successful? Or are they the figures of a company that is mature and stagnant, which finds it hard to generate additional income?

Then take a look at the brochures, promotional literature and website of your own business and those of your main competitors. Compare and contrast them. Are there degrees of professionalism between them? What are the underlying messages in all of them? Does one try to focus on low prices while another highlights added value?

Finally, check out your trade press and any relevant newspapers. What is really happening in your sector? Is it in for tough times or is a big expansion in the offing? Do your main competitors get a good write-up or no write-up at all?

Put all of these sources together. Make notes on them, scribble down your thoughts all over them and then put them in a big folder. You don't need to turn this into a major exercise, but it is important that you do this in order to get an idea of where you are in relation to the world outside.

Market research

Now we are getting into the realm of market research, but this really does not have to be as scary as it sounds. The thing to remember about all research, no matter which fancy titles academics may give it, is that it will fall into one of two categories: *quantitative* research and *qualitative* research. In simplistic terms, the role of qualitative research is to tell you *why*; quantitative research tells you *how many*. The methods are quite different and so are the answers, which is why it is important to think about the answers you want and how they will be used right at the beginning.

Qualitative research should be used when you really want to understand in detail why an individual does something. Qualitative research is particularly useful as a tool for determining *what* is important to people and *why* it is important.

Qualitative research should not be used when you need to learn how many people will respond in a particular way or how many hold a particular opinion. Qualitative research is not designed to collect quantifiable results. After learning why one person would respond in a certain way through qualitative research, it is relatively straightforward to count how many other individuals there are like that person through quantitative research.

The primary reason for conducting quantitative research is to learn how many people in a population have (or share) a particular characteristic or group of characteristics. But quantitative research is neither appropriate nor cost-effective for learning why people act or think as they do. The questions must be direct and easily quantified, and the sample must be quite large – 200 is an absolute minimum – so as to permit a reliable statistical analysis.

So far, however, you will have already collated a certain amount of quantitative data in the form of the literature you have analysed and any customer feedback systems you have. But now we are on a quest to find out people's opinions about you as a business. A very simple research plan that you will have at the end of this audit should look something like the one in the box below.

Quantitative research	*Qualitative research*
Sales	Employee opinion
Profit	Supplier opinion
Market share	Customer/client opinion
Customer feedback	Independent evaluation

This mix of primary (first-hand) and secondary ('desk') research will provide us with a useful background to define the problems and issues raised and give us the basis to analyse where your business is at present.

So what we will need to continue this audit is the following:

- a brief history of the firm;
- any written information regarding sales, profit, market share or customer surveys (which should now safely be in a big folder);
- employee attitudes;
- technological capabilities within the firm;
- a perception of where your business is within its marketplace.

The all-important point of 'a perception of where your business is within its marketplace', which is where the framing of a PR strategy comes in, will involve conversations with suppliers, employees, clients and distributors, as well as lumping in the information you provided as the owner-manager. This information will reveal critical weaknesses or strengths that we need to be aware of.

Questions, questions

It's time to get your pen out again! Below is a simple questionnaire for you to fill in so that we can get some basic information about your business:

Your firm's name:

How many people work in your firm?

When was it founded?

Where is your firm based?

How would you describe your firm's business sector and main market (eg business to business, business to consumer, national, international, European)?

How would you characterize your firm and how would you describe its main business focus?

Are you currently thinking about making any changes to your current business processes? If so, what are they?

Like it or hate it, technology is here to stay and is an important issue for the success of any small business. Study the following list and tick the ones that are appropriate to you.

What kind of computer technology do you have in your business?

We do not use computers

Single desktop/personal computer

Several stand-alone computers

Several computers sharing printers

Local area network ☐

Internet via modem ☐

Internet via ISDN ☐

Internet via broadband (DSL, ADSL) ☐

Non-internet wide area network (eg WAN) ☐

How often does your business use online services for the following purposes?

To review business opportunities and make bids for contracts ☐

To gather information/conduct research ☐

To communicate/send e-mail ☐

To transfer files and documents ☐

To showcase your products and services ☐

For e-commerce transactions ☐

To purchase products and services for your business ☐

To provide after-sales support ☐

Bookmark these pages, as you will probably keep referring to them. And just out of passing interest, take a look at what you put down about changing your business processes. Is there anything in the above list that you hadn't thought of that might help you make these processes easier?

Questions for others

The purpose of this section of the audit is to determine the perceptions of the effectiveness of your business with your suppliers, employees and clients (whether they are customers or distributors).

I'm afraid some more work is required here, but this will be the most strenuous exercise in this handbook and is very important, as it forms the basis of measuring where you are, so you can see how you have improved later on.

The only really effective method of collecting data about your reputation is through semi-structured telephone interviews of three groups: your suppliers, your employees and, of course, your customers. Your suppliers should be easy enough as, in effect, you are one of their customers so they should be only too pleased to help. Equally, your employees shouldn't be a problem. You should pick your customers at random – don't make them your 'best' customers as, obviously, they will only have good things to say about you!

You only need to pick *three* people from *each* category. The same interview schedule should be used in all cases. The idea is simply to get a snapshot of the business, so write a simple summary paragraph for each answer outlining the main comments.

Section one – suppliers

Question 1: 'How important is [your business name] to you?'

```
┌─────────────────────────────────────────────┐
│                                               │
│                                               │
│                                               │
│                                               │
└─────────────────────────────────────────────┘
```

Question 2: 'How well does [your business name] interact with you?'

```
┌─────────────────────────────────────────────┐
│                                               │
│                                               │
│                                               │
└─────────────────────────────────────────────┘
```

Question 3: 'With regard to [your business name], how effective are they?'

```

```

Question 4: 'With regard to [your business name], how efficient are they?'

```

```

Question 5: 'How do they compare with similar businesses that you have contact with?'

```

```

Section two – employees

Question 1: 'What is [your business name] like to work for?'

```

```

Question 2: 'With regard to [your business name], how effective are they?'

```

```

Question 3: 'With regard to [your business name], how efficient are they?'

```
┌──────────────────────────────────────────────────┐
│                                                    │
│                                                    │
│                                                    │
│                                                    │
└──────────────────────────────────────────────────┘
```

Question 4: 'How do they compare with similar businesses that you have contact with?'

```
┌──────────────────────────────────────────────────┐
│                                                    │
│                                                    │
│                                                    │
│                                                    │
└──────────────────────────────────────────────────┘
```

Section three – customers

Question 1: 'How important is [your business name] to you?'

```
┌──────────────────────────────────────────────────┐
│                                                    │
│                                                    │
│                                                    │
│                                                    │
└──────────────────────────────────────────────────┘
```

Question 2: 'How well does [your business name] interact with you?'

```
┌──────────────────────────────────────────────────┐
│                                                    │
│                                                    │
│                                                    │
│                                                    │
└──────────────────────────────────────────────────┘
```

Question 3: 'With regard to [your business name], how effective are they?'

```
┌──────────────────────────────────────────────────┐
│                                                    │
│                                                    │
│                                                    │
│                                                    │
└──────────────────────────────────────────────────┘
```

Question 4: 'With regard to [your business name], how efficient are they?'

```
┌──────────────────────────────────────────────────────────┐
│                                                            │
│                                                            │
│                                                            │
│                                                            │
│                                                            │
└──────────────────────────────────────────────────────────┘
```

Question 5: 'How do they compare with similar businesses that you have contact with?'

```
┌──────────────────────────────────────────────────────────┐
│                                                            │
│                                                            │
│                                                            │
│                                                            │
│                                                            │
└──────────────────────────────────────────────────────────┘
```

General comment on findings

Now write a very general comment about the way these three groups appear to perceive your company.

```
┌──────────────────────────────────────────────────────────┐
│                                                            │
│                                                            │
│                                                            │
│                                                            │
│                                                            │
└──────────────────────────────────────────────────────────┘
```

Quick recap

You have just done a good audit of your own business. You should now have a useful snapshot of your business, your customers, your reputation, your aspirations and any PR you have done in the past. You will also have a good idea of the way the outside world perceives your business: firstly, through things that have already been written and, secondly, through the first-hand opinions of people who are key to the success of your business. You will have a better idea of two other key areas as well: how your competitors are perceived; and the capabilities of your business when looking at changing direction in order to make more profits. It really is important that you have addressed this section well, as it will all come together when you start creating your 'master strategy' in Chapter 2!

Case study ═══════════════════════════════════

The product

Ten collectable, 3.5-centimetre-high interactive pets that respond to voice-activated commands.

The challenge

Each year, approximately 50,000 new toys are launched – all vying for media and consumers' attention and aiming to be among the top toys for Christmas. The PR challenge was to turn Tomy's new MicroPets range into a collectable craze that would make them one of the best-selling toys of 2002.

Objectives

- To make MicroPets the hottest, most innovative toy product for 2002.
- To establish MicroPets as the most talked-about toy in 2002.
- To assist in creating a kids' craze for Christmas 2003.
- To position MicroPets as cool and collectable among kids aged 6–10 years.

Execution and implementation

The PR campaign was designed to achieve three different goals:

- *Pre-launch:* to establish word-of-mouth and playground buzz.
- *The launch:* to announce the availability of MicroPets to the UK media and consumers.
- *The build:* to maintain a consistently high profile for MicroPets in the run-up to Christmas.

Pre-launch

The pre-launch campaign kicked off with a sneak preview of MicroPets to a handful of opinion-forming journalists who were invited to a private room at the Toy Fair trade show in the spring of 2002.

To tap into the Japanese technological reputation, the PR team organized a live webcast from the Japanese Toy Fair in May. A Japanese presenter was used to give the product 'authenticity' and street cred. Over 300 media were sent a mailer to invite them to log on to see the launch.

A series of one-to-one media previews was given in Japanese-themed locations including Nobu and Yo!Sushi to build interest prior to launch and secure major editorial features.

A 'miniature' mailer inside the toy's packaging was sent to all relevant youth, gadget and national media but no product. In order to get their hands on a MicroPet, media had to contact the press office, enabling them to create a database of 'MicroPets mates'.

Finally, the toys were unveiled to over 200 journalists at a July press conference held in Attenborough Associates' offices (AA Ltd).

Launch and build

All relevant media received a MicroPet on the day of the launch. From July onwards, releases and photography were fed to the media that capitalized on topical stories. These included:

- *July* – MicroPets playing on a Subbuteo football pitch to tie in with the World Cup;
- *August* – release based on Japanese miniature trends including micro-scooters;
- *September* – MicroPets on a sushi plate in Yo!Sushi;
- *October* – a MicroPet in the mouth of a Japanese sumo wrestler;
- *November* – the Race of the MicroPets, pitting character against character;
- *December* – announcing a shortage of MicroPets and emergency new shipments.

AA Ltd approached *The Guinness Book of Records* to persuade them to agree a world record for the smallest interactive toy. This was exploited as an opportunity for a December photocall (the *Sun* and the *Daily Star*) and an additional news story.

Working closely with Hamleys and an independent toy seller in Bournemouth, they leaked the 'news' that MicroPets was the best-selling toy for Christmas. This was accompanied by a photocall with cute children with their pets and a quote from toy retailers talking about the demand for the product.

The ongoing PR campaign helped to encourage the British Association for Toy Retailers to choose MicroPets as one of the Top 10 Toys, further guaranteeing MicroPets a place on Christmas present lists. On announcement day, AA Ltd ensured that every relevant TV programme had a set to demonstrate.

TV programmes included CiTV, *RI:SE*, *Richard & Judy*, *The Saturday Show* and *Milkshake*, which were all targeted in the months before Christmas to maintain a TV presence up until the big day.

Evaluation and measurement

Within a month of the summer launch, MicroPets had become a best-selling toy, helped by widespread publicity that then continued to grow in the run-up to Christmas.

MicroPets achieved blanket national coverage (appearing at least once in every daily national newspaper including the *Financial Times*) over the course of the nine-month campaign. Media coverage also encompassed many weekend newspapers and supplements, more than 200 regional newspapers, over 70 radio stations, 30 children's titles and 20 websites. The toys were shown on 14 television programmes including ITN and *Sky News*. The combined audience exceeded 95 million.

There were also nine features in the toy trade press to maintain interest from retailers in MicroPets. MicroPets' sales success is the ultimate testament to a strong PR campaign. Tomy reported sales of 1 million units in 2002 at a retail value of £10 million. MicroPets were voted 'Best New Product of the Year 2002' by the British Association of Toy Retailers.

Strategy versus tactics

Before we go any further we need to discuss the whole idea of a 'strategy'. The word 'strategy' is used a lot and, when there is a particularly big problem, then organizations will say that they are drawing up a 'detailed strategy' in order to deal with it. In reality, however, strategies should never be detailed: a strategy should be simple. It's the way that the objectives of the strategy are achieved – the *tactics* – that are usually the complicated and imaginative part.

The rest of this section will deal with war. This doesn't mean I want you to go out and hire the A-Team in order to blow up your competitors. But the whole idea of strategy and tactics is steeped in the history of the battlefield. If you look up 'strategy' in the dictionary, you will get something like: 'The science of military command, or the science of projecting campaigns and directing great military movements; generalship.'

If you look up 'tactics' in that same dictionary, you should see something along the lines of: 'The science and art of disposing military and naval forces in order for battle, and performing military and naval evolutions. It is divided into grand tactics, or the tactics of battles, and elementary tactics, or the tactics of instruction. Hence, any system or method of procedure.'

We need to clearly define the difference between strategy and tactics. In this way, when analysing a problem, we will rapidly realize which category things fall into.

Strategy is almost always long-term planning. It involves all those things that you'll need to worry about for a long time. Formulating your strategy must have as its final goal your total and unquestionable 'victory'. If not, then the strategy is incomplete.

With this ultimate goal in mind, you must ask yourself the question: 'What stands in my way?'

A military strategy would begin with the following format:

- Understand your mission.
- Get your starting territories (your audit). Analyse which ones are 'weak' (isolated, all alone) and which ones are 'strong' (grouped with other of your territories or in a good position; control of Malaysia *and* Indonesia, for example, is key to conquering Australia!).
- Formulate a plan to complete your mission given the placement of your territories.
- Place your armies in the best manner possible to execute your plan.
- Analyse the other players' positions and try to determine *their* missions from *their* stance.

From this, your plan should be simple and flexible enough to encompass most probable outcomes (possible alliances, definite enemies, highly contested and less contested territories, etc) and lead you to victory. This plan, in brief, is your strategy.

Tactics, on the other hand, are often improvised. They are short-term plans, usually occurring only in combat. Their improvised nature stems from the unpredictability of conflict. By its very nature, a plan that says 'Right, we'll storm up the right flank and then smash the centre from behind' is a strategy. A plan such as 'Look, they're running! *Chaaarge!*' is a tactic.

But don't get this wrong: tactics don't have to be dumb and strategies smart. Something as simple as 'I'll deprive my opponent of resources' is, if not your strategy, an element of your strategy (and you can make it 90 per cent of your strategy). Despite a tactic being usually improvised, you can come to know and understand when to use a specific one. Again, this requires analysing your competitor's strengths and weaknesses, the positioning of your 'forces', and timing!

So to recap, definitions of strategy and tactics are:

- *strategy: planning for the big picture;*
- tactics: creating and exploiting opportunities when they arise.

This is war!

It is widely accepted that, after their defeat in the Second World War, the Japanese were the first to embrace the ideal of 'business is war'. This means that business uses the ideas of the battlefield and applies them to the world of business. And it certainly worked for Japan: today, Japan is a major or dominant power in almost every world strategic industry including finance, communications, mass transit, semiconductors, motor vehicles and popular entertainment. The world's largest banks are all Japanese. The largest record company in the United States is Japanese, and two of the three biggest movie and entertainment companies in the United States are Japanese. Many big companies in the US, like Loews Theatres, Firestone Tires and 7-Eleven, are also Japanese. In fact, 7 of the 10 largest companies in the world are Japanese. Furthermore, Japan today is the world's biggest manufacturer of cars, having surpassed the United States in the mid-1980s. These were all US-dominated industries 25 years ago.

Believe it or not, this phenomenal success can be traced back to ancient China, in particular a great military general named Sun Tzu. It is reckoned that he lived from around 544 BC to 496 BC in the ancient state of Ch'i.

Sun Tzu wrote the earliest – and still the most revered – military strategy book in the world. This masterpiece is best known to most of us as *The Art of War* and can be found on the shelves of most good bookshops. Since naming a written work after its author was customary in ancient China, the text was originally referred to as simply 'Sun Tzu'. Skilled and experienced in warfare matters during a time of unprecedented political turmoil, Sun Tzu presented his treatise to King Ho-lu of the Wu state. The sovereign was impressed. When asked whether its principles could be applied to anyone, Sun Tzu replied, 'Yes.' As proof of his competency and to confirm the principles' effectiveness, he successfully transformed 180 court women into trained soldiers in just one session.

With Sun Tzu as general, King Ho-lu captured the capital city of Ying to defeat the powerful Ch'u state in 506 BC. They then headed north and subdued Ch'i and Chin. Not surprisingly, Sun Tzu's name quickly spread throughout the land and among the feudal lords.

How he later lived or died is unknown. However, it was declared that, '10 miles outside the city gate of Wu Hsieh, there is a large tomb of the great strategist Sun Tzu'. By the Han dynasty, his reputation as a wise and respected military leader was well known. Considering the countless texts lost or destroyed throughout China's history, the remarkable survival and relevancy of Sun Tzu's *The Art of War* to this very day attest to its immeasurable value.

This fact was not lost on the Japanese. Sun Tzu was first introduced to Japan as early as AD 400. Japan's leaders earnestly applied Sun Tzu to warfare: the samurai would peruse its contents before each battle. They were among the most diligent practitioners of the book's concepts and came up with their own term to encapsulate its meaning: Sonshi.

I'm sure your business would like one day to be the same size as your average *keiretsu* (almost all the significant companies in Japan are aligned in one of about six *keiretsus* or business 'groupings'. These are loosely linked 'super-corporations' for lack of a better term. Most of the Japanese companies whose brands we know and love are in these *keiretsus*. Several of these *keiretsus* have been around a very long time (before the Second World War) dating back to feudal-like family-run trading houses. Mitsubishi and Mitsui are two of the more famous ones. Famous companies like Nissan, Toshiba and Sumitomo Bank are all in *keiretsus*). If you want to win your own war, then PR will be an important part of your strategy. How it all fits together will be explored now.

How to win...

To give you more of an idea of what a strategy looks like, we'll explore ways in which you can achieve success with military precision. Firstly, we take the idea of 'strategic directions'. Every strategy (which we will construct over the following chapters of this book) will have a general direction that it will go in. So how do you go about deciding on the right PR approach? Which strategy and tactics package best suits the particular needs of your communications campaign?

Niche defence

For 'niche strategy', read 'playing to your strengths'. In other words, talk about what you know while at the same time highlighting exactly why you're the best at what you do.

This is largely a method for businesses that deal in highly specialized products or services – such as the IT sector. It is particularly effective if you're much better at what you do than your competitors. Remember, your actions are as important as your messages, so you must be sure of your facts before playing the niche card.

For example, if you're Microsoft and you've got the market cornered, it's fairly straightforward to begin all of your PR propositions with the statement 'We're the best at what we do.' But what if you're a smaller company? Well, perhaps your strengths lie in customer service, a genuinely innovative hi-tech product, knowledgeable and friendly staff or strongly held and acted upon environmental principles, or maybe you've just implemented that key idea that really differentiates your service from the competition.

Whatever your niche might be, it is important to tell people about it and tell them consistently – sounds obvious but you'd be surprised at how many companies miss out on this simple action. Bring out the key areas in which your business excels and then communicate these unique selling points (USPs) as part of an encompassing corporate image or tie them into a specific communications campaign.

Territorial defence

Does it ever seem to you these days that nearly everything is becoming bigger, 'better' and more centralized than ever before? The high street is dying – long live the mega retail parks, often run by anonymous shareholders in a distant country! OK, a little cynical maybe, but this backdrop does offer a chance for small businesses to get customers onside in their fight against the mega corp.

In general the territorial defence is most commonly used by smaller businesses that have a specialist focus within a limited community. These companies often promote their 'human' face when dealing with customers, and communication campaigns lead with individuals or people issues that a target audience can easily relate to.

Businesses using this approach often utilize corporate social responsibility (CSR) programmes, highlighting strong ties with local, social or charity-based issues that impact upon relevant decision makers and customers.

The strategy hinges on your business being able to show excellent development and sustainability in a local marketplace. Reputation, regional knowledge and community relations are of paramount importance. It is still possible for the territorial defence to work for bigger companies – think of international banker HSBC's recent ad campaign in which it tells us its huge size and success are largely due to specialist local knowledge in countries around the world.

Blocking attack

This plan of action effectively 'does what it says on the tin' by blocking competitors from gaining access to key market segments, affiliates or distribution channels. To achieve this it is necessary to expand your own product or service range into a 'one-stop-shop' format that effectively supplies everything a customer, affiliate or distributor requires.

An established and genuine corporate approach on your company's part to customer feedback is vital here. Establish procedures to allow for both customer and staff feedback and use this information to develop company policies on the what, where and when of your products and services.

Blocking attacks are usually used by customer-led businesses against competitors that focus on niche or small market segments. Your customer-centric approach will mean that you are better at listening to your clients, identifying their needs and moving quickly into action to satisfy them. Your customers will directly influence your core business plan and this will be the secret of your success.

Guerrilla PR

In recent years so-called 'guerrilla PR' has become increasingly popular because of its swift, hard-hitting methods and results. It also often steals the glory from under the noses of competitors who may have already invested substantially in a more traditional approach to PR and marketing.

As an example of this, think of Coca-Cola spending millions of dollars on TV rights for a nationally broadcast football game. They have their branding in place around the stadium, their sponsor messages during breaks in the TV coverage and maybe even their logo emblazoned on players' outfits. Then, at the last moment, a team from Pepsi arrive at the stadium entrance and give every fan they can a free giant foam finger-pointing hand – emblazoned with the Pepsi logo – to help cheer their team along. Now every time the camera pans the crowd the viewers at home get to do their own taste test – Pepsi spend a few thousand dollars against Coca-Cola's millions and still get their message across.

Such results can also make for a fun news piece and will most likely leave your competitors feeling furious they hadn't thought of it first. Another useful ploy is to release last-minute updates to customers via e-mail, detailing your next guerrilla campaign.

Full attack

Remember the lawnmower wars of the mid-1980s? Qualcast repeatedly told us that a Hover mower was a lot of 'bovver', while Hover countered that if they weren't so damn good their competitors wouldn't be quite so 'bovvered' about them.

The most important point to remember with the full attack is that war is never pretty and at the end of the day someone always gets hurt. This is all about taking the gloves off and going straight for your competitor's jugular. You will publicly attack its products, service, record and standing. The approach requires both nerve and detailed legal consultation. It's also worth remembering that once you start down this route and pick a fight it can be very difficult to turn back.

Further to this, and as any good politician will tell you, overly negative campaigning can sometimes end up being more damaging to the initiator than to the target. Before launching into a full attack be sure to:

- get your facts straight;
- cover all possible contingencies for the inevitable comeback;
- use the opportunity effectively to highlight why your products or services are both different from and better than those offered by your target;
- if the situation allows, use humour to help convey your message (no one likes people who take themselves too seriously);
- be prepared for a battle of attrition;
- have plenty of money in the bank!

Flanking attack

There's nothing quite so harsh as hitting people when they're down, but then again what works works. The flanking attack is all about identifying an opponent's weaknesses and exploiting them. Soon you will carry out a 'strengths, weaknesses, opportunities and threats' (SWOT) analysis of your own business – so ensure that you apply the same methodology to your competitors.

Identifying that spot where a competitor is significantly weak allows you to highlight why your product or service is clearly superior. In addition, if a flanking attack is carried out effectively it can also force your opponent to divert valuable resources to help protect the newly highlighted weakness. This in turn starts to make the opponent weaker in other areas, and so on and so on.

The approach is all about taking the initiative and keeping your opponent constantly on the back foot. Perhaps your best business propositions are on price, service or specialist knowledge – play to these strengths strategically against the weaknesses of others, and be careful to ensure your own house is fully in order to help safeguard against potential counter-attacks.

Mobile defence

Keeping your business consistently ahead of the competition is an ideal goal. The mobile defence is specially tailored for this and is akin to being in a state of permanent innovation. The strategy is particularly employed in the hi-tech and convenience sectors, which rely heavily on research and the development of 'fast-moving goods'. The ideal result is a rapid turnover that keeps your company afloat.

However, be warned. Mobile defence is based on a potentially hazardous 'sink or swim' scenario. The prospective rewards are high if a company has the vision, resources and reputation to manage the job. But it is important that innovation is genuine, as key messages to both potential and existing customers must match the reality of the situation – otherwise you will quickly be found out.

In terms of communication and publicizing your success, the job is made all the easier as 'new' equals 'news'. Keep the stories on this front churning out and your reputation as a market leader will be assured.

Stealth defence

Sometimes it's just good to talk. Formalized PR and marketing communication campaigns can be costly, but by deliberately avoiding the limelight normally associated with a really great business idea, word of mouth may prove just the ticket for your promotional needs.

The stealth approach can also serve to keep your competitors in the dark as to exactly what you are doing, while freeing up valuable cash that can be invested directly back into products and services. You also create an underground 'buzz' about your product or service, guarding it like a precious secret that only a privileged few have access to. This mystique opens options on premium pricing and the potential for developing connections with key high-end markets.

To support this image you will need to develop an exclusive 'club' format for your products. Websites may need to be password protected, and membership for your best customers will become a prerequisite.

Diplomatic nous

Partnering up with significant third-party players can be a good thing. While basking in the glory of an established company's already glowing reputation for high standards of delivery and service, you can also generate more commercial punching power. All of this will be largely on the back of a business that will have done much of the hard work and promotional spending for you.

One example of this process took place recently when a small Scottish materials business producing Harris tweed received a substantial order from sports apparel giant Nike. The request massively multiplied production requirements of the niche fabric for use in a new range of women's athletic shoes. The story quickly went global and, because of the inequality in size between the two businesses and the novelty factor of 'old meets new', the story gained enormous international coverage and breathed new life into the small materials company.

Diplomatic nous is often employed by innovative and enterprising smaller companies that are more than willing to negotiate with bigger partners while looking for quick growth routes. This association can sometimes be achieved by securing licensing or distribution deals.

Joint licensing of this kind inevitably leads to joint PR programmes. Competent lines of communication on agreed promotional strategy and sign-off procedures for campaigns and tactics need to be set in place and agreed at the earliest opportunity.

Surround and drown

This strategy is effectively about surrounding a competing product or service in a sea of your own promotional offers and special deals and then dragging it out into increasingly deep water until it drowns. It is important to isolate your target through the production of a flood of comparably favourable offers, products and associated features – all of which should result in customers veritably stampeding away from your target and into your welcoming arms.

This approach is often employed in relatively mature markets against long-term brand leaders that have become complacent with regards to their positioning and belief in the unchanging loyalty of their core customer base.

Differentiation between your own business proposition and that of your competitors is vital, as is the communication of your innovative and fresh perspective in a possibly jaded market.

Surround and drown is ideal for use against the niche business, by bombarding its long-term customers with a fresh range of options on price and choice. An everyday example of this process is the successful growth through diversification of the major supermarket chains, which regularly surround and drown small town retailers. A long-term PR approach full of variety and adaptability is a prerequisite here.

Example

Let's take the classic small-business scenario. You are operating in a competitive market that is dominated by a particularly big competitor. Let's look at your situation. Your business offers flexibility and individual customer service. You are innovative and have a good territorial advantage as you are a well-known local company. However, you constantly have to be on your toes because your big competitor has the resources to push its bigger product range, which is often cheaper than yours because it can buy and stock larger quantities.

What do you do? Well, you regard your territorial advantage as the most important one, so you go for a 'territorial defence'. You step up local delivery times, making them slicker than ever. You make your offerings more appealing to local customers, breeding community loyalty. And all of this is communicated through a PR campaign that creates a community flavour.

Bearing all this in mind, the strategic direction that you chose for your own business was:

Congratulations again! You have just carefully outlined some key business objectives, and you're well on the way to becoming a great general! These business objectives are vital as they will be the whole reason behind having a PR campaign at all. They will be the drivers that will move your business in the direction that you want it to go. All we need now is a smooth-running PR campaign...

2 Why you need PR

Introduction

In this chapter we will explore why PR is so important to small business success. Contrary to most areas where small businesses compete with their larger cousins, this is one that small businesses should find easy and win every time. It will show what forces are at work when undertaking PR, and why good PR, for small businesses, can be the most effective promotional activity they can undertake, while at the same time being the least expensive.

What's so good about PR?

The rather formal description of PR (as issued by the Chartered Institute of Public Relations) is about 'influencing behaviour to achieve objectives through the effective management of relationships and communications'.

What this really boils down to is creating a 'buzz' about your organization. It's about putting together a strategy to turbocharge awareness and demand for you and your services, and finding new ways to highlight 'must-have' features about your business by using independent press and credible third-party views.

And this is not just a 'pie-in-the-sky' ideal. You can create a 'buzz' by doing, for example, these relatively easy and straightforward things:

- forming strategic alliances with appropriate small-business partners to back up the credibility and authority of your brand;
- producing newsletters with useful information to small firms and contributors from high-profile third parties;
- conducting cost-effective research surveys by negotiating them to be run in conjunction with leading publications;
- hitting high press coverage targets in national, regional, online and specialist media;
- securing early, heavyweight media endorsement and endorsement from analysts in order to inform and lead debate;
- creating word-of-mouth buzz by tapping into existing publicity vehicles in the business community;
- using a whole host of other public relations tactics to generate 'creative standout' within your sector.

This all might sound a bit daunting, but it really isn't. I used the word 'strategy' earlier on, and at this point you may be thinking 'Oh, no, another big strategy document they want you to write. I don't know how, and I don't have time!' Well, actually, your strategy in PR will be the same as everyone else's, from Findus through to the chip shop. You want to:

- raise your brand awareness among your key audiences;
- communicate messages to these audiences;
- differentiate yourself from the competition;
- position yourself as an authoritative industry voice with an in-depth understanding of your market.

And how do you achieve this Holy Grail? Well, you have to:

1. identify your *relevant target audiences*;
2. identify the best ways to reach your *relevant target audiences*;
3. gain *positive exposure* within your audiences;
4. communicate *key messages* to these audiences; and
5. gain a leading *'share of voice'* compared with your competitors.

At the end of the day, it's all about achieving *outcomes* by increasing awareness, influencing attitudes and – vitally – *changing behaviour*.

So it is well within your grasp to change your business for the better in ways you can only begin to imagine.

The two-way symmetric model

Using this model successfully is what most businesses strive for, and if you can get this right then you're well on your way to being ICI, Virgin and BT all rolled into one! The two-way symmetric model is all about a free and equal information flow between an organization and its target audiences, leading to mutual understanding and responsiveness. This may result in *either* the organization *or* its audiences being persuaded to change their position. But the model is regarded as equally effective if neither group changes, 'as long as both communicate well enough to understand the position of the other', as James E Grunig says. And he should know: he's published over 150 articles, books, chapters, papers and reports on the subject, and Greenlee School chairman John Eighmey said: 'Jim Grunig's accomplishments transcend public relations theory and practice. His theories, research findings and recommendations for the effective practice of public relations are admired and utilized by public relations scholars and practitioners on a worldwide basis.'

So 'two-way symmetric' PR is about gaining mutual understanding, striking up a balanced, two-way communication, and using feedback to adjust what you are doing or at least to be happy that your key audiences know *why* you are doing what you are doing.

So why do we do it?

Why do we go through all this hassle? If I sell tables, then surely I just put an advert in the newspaper and people who need a table come to me and buy one? Actually, this was how things started out. In the 1800s, 'to advertise' meant to disseminate news: so newspapers that call themselves the *Advertiser* originally carried a lot of news, not a lot of adverts. It would be common for an advert in a newspaper to read 'Colin Smith, seller of tables'. This was announcing that, if you were in the market for a table, then Colin Smith was your man. The idea of persuading people who might not think they need a table to go out and purchase one is most definitely a phenomenon of recent times.

The fact is that the game has changed. PR is simply about understanding this game and getting your target audiences to change on a number of levels:

- to inform them about what you do ('cognitive change': a fancy way of saying that they now understand what you do and what you do differently);
- to get them to use what you provide (action change);
- to get them to continue to use what you provide (behavioural change);
- to convince them that they really are continually getting the best deal from you, and not just in monetary terms (value change).

PR is a lot of things, but there are also things that it is not. PR is often confused with advertising, merchandising, promotion or any of a dozen other buzz words in the marketing communications vocabulary. But PR is actually about doing something newsworthy that you want to communicate and then telling your target audience what you have done. At the same time, however, it is a very important part of your marketing strategy. Let me explain...

Advertising is very different from public relations. One key difference is that you always pay for the space and time of an advertisement (or commercial appearing on radio, television or the internet). By contrast, editorial coverage generated through public relations is not paid for by the business. The media will pick up and publish the story because they consider it newsworthy, not as a paid advertisement.

But a crucial difference is that, in advertising, you have virtually full control over the message. Because you are paying for advertising, the ad or commercial runs your exact text (called 'copy'), provided the copy complies with generally acceptable standards for advertising.

In the case of public relations, the media outlet you are targeting is under no obligation to run the story in any form. If a media outlet does decide to run the story, an editor will generally rewrite the news release or use pertinent information from the news release to create the news. In addition, you have no control over when the release or news will run. All decisions are made by the editor.

So things are not always straightforward. As you can see, public relations is a cost-effective way of getting your story out. But it has to be handled properly: taking the trouble to write effective news releases and to build a relationship with the relevant media will, in time, pay dividends in the form of exposure and prestige. Best of all, public relations usually costs less than a single advertisement.

Since public relations communicates your messages through the news media, all the power of the media is brought to bear when the public – those viewers, listeners or readers you want to reach – learn about your news. Think of what this means: high interest level, credibility, implied objectivity and possibly implied endorsement by the journalist or publication reporting the information. There is also an urgency conveyed when news is reported in the media, and that news has the potential to reach a tremendously large audience.

With exposure comes awareness. An important goal of public relations – in any medium – is to make people aware of what your organization is, what it offers and what it does. Never underestimate the value of such awareness. In flashier terms, it's called *buzz*.

Creating awareness for your organization means that you must inform your key audiences about what you offer and how you can meet their needs. Public relations is probably the most valuable tool in accomplishing this. A well-implemented public relations initiative will help present your organization's offerings to their best advantage.

Public and news media relations also position you to enter new marketplaces and expose new products or services to new audiences – all without the expense associated with an advertising programme. A sustained public relations programme allows you to ensure your offerings are in front of appropriate decision makers. This continuous flow of information creates a constant awareness and a constant influx of inquiries – especially when integrated with other powerful marketing communications tools such as brochures, trade shows and so on.

And linking PR activities with your marketing activities can have serious benefits. For example, a car manufacturer wanted to launch a new model among potential buyers, using both advertising and PR. From a consumer sample, two research groups were identified: those who had read the publications in which PR media coverage appeared (such as magazine reviews), seen TV programmes that reviewed the car and so on (the 'PR exposed'); and those who had only seen the advertisements ('non-PR exposed').

After eight weeks of the campaign, the results shown in Figure 2.1 were found.

Evidence showed that PR caused a big and widening gap between the PR 'exposed' and the 'non-exposed', meaning that the TV advertisements were much more effective when used alongside a PR campaign. Analysis by the research firm Millward Brown Précis established that heightened awareness was not caused by other marketplace activity.

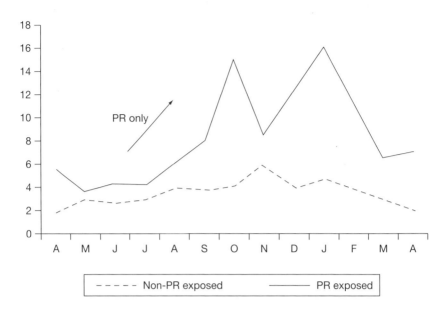

Figure 2.1 Spontaneous brand awareness of new launch

A smaller rise in awareness was noticed among the non-exposed slightly after the advertising. This was attributed to the fact that, although not PR exposed themselves, they had been influenced by those who were exposed – the 'buzz effect'. The 'exposed' had much higher levels of awareness, almost certainly as a result of the combination of PR and advertising.

In another example, a food product was supported by both PR and advertising. At the start of the campaign there was a much higher level of purchase by the 'exposed' group, but when the first TV advertising burst kicked in the 'non-exposed' caught up – again the result of the 'buzz effect' (see Figure 2.2). The subsequent rise among the 'exposed', coinciding with the second TV advertising burst, was explained by the fact that the two advertisements were different. The second one was in line with the PR message, resulting in an effect of a coherent message and more sales.

All this is saying in a roundabout way is that marketing is much more successful when it is being backed up by a PR campaign. One cannot really exist without the other (well, it can, but as we've seen not as successfully). That's why this handbook will show you how to fit a PR strategy into what your organization is already doing.

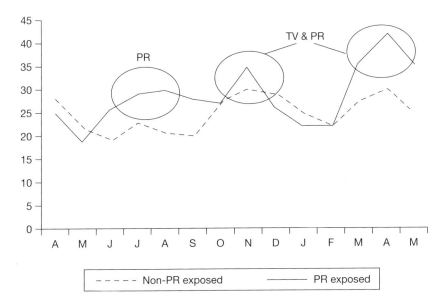

Figure 2.2 Likelihood of buying

Case study

Background

Thule is a manufacturer of car roof accessories. Their PR agency, Publicity Matters, was faced with the need to create maximum noise and widespread coverage for the new product, with the constraint of a minimal budget. Publicity Matters suggested launching the Evolution on the internet.

Objectives

Thule defined three simple objectives:
1. to raise awareness of the new Evolution roof box in order to maximize sales;
2. to communicate the product qualities of Evolution – aerodynamic, stylish and cost-effective;
3. to attack different markets other than the typical 'male ABC' roof box purchaser.

With this in mind Publicity Matters researched and established a target audience and created an appropriate media list.

Plan and strategy

Publicity Matters knew that trying to entice London motoring journalists to travel to Somerset would be near impossible. The alternative, a London-based event, would have been costly and not necessarily distinctive. By using the internet as the location, journalists would not even have to leave their desks. Publicity Matters costed up a three-stage campaign that would be viable within the budget: a teaser campaign; the launch; and maintaining momentum.

Execution and implementation

Pre-launch

National motoring journalists were sent a teaser that led them to a page on the website. The idea was to maintain secrecy of what Thule was claiming was the most technically advanced roof box available in the world, while stimulating interest in the media. Once at the site the journalist would discover various video clips of people waiting for something, such as a clock ticking, someone waiting at traffic lights and a father waiting for the birth of a baby. There was also a counter to the launch day.

A week before the launch, the same media list was sent a champagne invitation to attend the UK's first automotive virtual press launch, followed by an e-mail reminder three days before the launch. Selected journalists from key publications were supplied embargoed information to be released on the day of the launch.

The launch

On the day, a targeted list received comprehensive media packs that included various photography, technical specifications and Thule background information.

At 11 am exactly, the launch took place. Viewers who logged on were greeted with an exciting loading screen, followed by a short 'Flash' video detailing the benefits of the product. Every conceivable feature of the box was covered in a series of 30-second videos, with downloadable fact sheets of information. The journalists' interest was further stimulated with a competition to win a roof box, which was only available to journalists from the invited publications. At 4 pm on the site, the competition winner was announced, encouraging further hits on the site from the audience.

Post-launch

A number of publications ran reader competitions. Journalists who visited the site on the day were offered a roof box to test; many of these tests were featured the following months. All publications received follow-up calls and were offered further information regarding Thule products.

Results and evaluation

Without the cost of a venue, catering and other costs associated with a press launch, Publicity Matters kept within the tight budget. Thule's website normally receives 1,200 hits a month. Between 11 am and 11.20 on 1 March the website received 800 unique hits in 20 minutes. A number of motoring publications were supplied embargoed information and ran product details on launch day. Magazines such as *What Car?*, *Auto Express* and *Top Gear* ran reader competitions. The Evolution was also tested by journalists from magazines that had never before covered Thule, such as *Practical Caravanning* and *Yachting World*.

The client felt that the results achieved by the launch were exceptional. The press coverage of the Thule Evolution achieved a total combined readership of 6,696,694. Since the launch, the Thule website has had more hits than ever before. Publicity Matters has received recognition in a number of business and trade publications for its innovative approach.

PR Week and *Business Update* ran case studies proving how the internet is benefiting geographically constrained companies such as Thule and Publicity Matters. Most importantly, sales figures at the end of April showed a twofold increase and the Evolution rapidly sold out in a number of stores around the country.

What is PR about then?

PR is actually a discipline with quite an in-depth history. It has a whole mass of theories behind it, which are briefly outlined here:

- Theories of relationships:
  - *System theory:* evaluates relationships and structure as they relate to the whole.
  - *Situational theory:* situations define relationships.
  - *Approaches to conflict resolution:* includes separating people from the problem; focusing on interests, not positions; inventing options for mutual gain; and insisting on objective criteria.
- Theories of cognition and behaviour:
  - *Action assembly theory:* understanding behaviour by understanding how people think.
  - *Social exchange theory:* predicting behaviour of groups and individuals based on perceived rewards and costs.
  - *Diffusion theory:* people adopt an important idea or innovation after going through five discrete steps – awareness, interest, evaluation, trial and adoption.

- *Social learning theory:* people use information processing to explain and predict behaviour.
- *Elaborated likelihood model:* suggests decision making is influenced through repetition, rewards and credible spokespersons.
- Theories of mass communication:
  - *Uses and gratification:* people are active users of media and select media based on the gratification for them.
  - *Agenda-setting theory:* suggests that the media content that people read, see and listen to sets the agenda for society's discussion and interaction.

Although the above might sound quite academic and convoluted, if not a little fragmented as well, the following section aims to show you what it means in practice and how it all fits together.

How does PR work?

PR is not *just* about dealing effectively with the media: there is far more to it than that. PR can do exciting things with what you have to offer. For example, eBay.com's founders boasted that they spent no money on advertising apart from PR for two years. Pierre Omidyar, founder and chairman, said: 'Advertising is not necessarily the most effective way of building a solid group of [customers]. We're more interested in reaching out to people through grassroots efforts. We'll build... by listening to the community. If you advertise a lot before building your business, that's just shouting from the rooftops.'

PR is really about *communication* and how effectively you do it. The effectiveness of communication is dependent on a number of key factors. These include how communicators look in relation to their respective position of status, value, competence, honesty, reliability and credibility. Beyond these personal elements, the next key factors are the way you get your message across together with the style and content of the communication.

So the first thing you have to do is answer the following questions. What kind of an organization do you want to be? What do you want to do?

Well, what you *don't* want is simply to be an organization steeped in reactive public relations. This is based on an organization as something called a 'closed system', which only stirs into life when the system is disturbed. These types of systems are designed to deflect outside forces away from the organization (see Figure 2.3), rather than letting outside forces change the organization. It has been estimated that 85 per cent of organizations practise public relations in this way.

But the outside world is constantly changing, and you need to keep pace with external changes: what we need to do is actually to capitalize on opportunities and seek *advantages* through these changes. The way to do this is to forge a genuine two-way relationship with your key audiences.

Your business operates in an increasingly complex and ever-changing environment, and outside pressures – not just commercial ones – affect your organization on many differing levels, which are all inter-related (see Figure 2.4).

You cannot control this environment, nor can you control the hearts and minds of the people you need to influence. What you can and should do, however, is to create a mutual understanding between

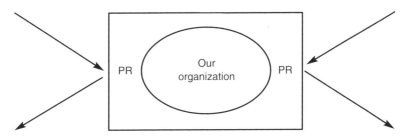

Figure 2.3   Deflecting outside forces

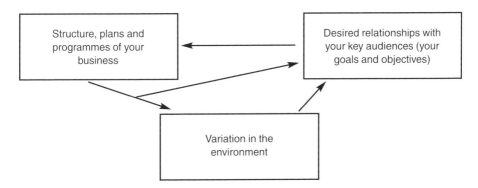

Figure 2.4   Pressures affecting the organization

yourself as an organization and the players that you need to influence. You need to communicate with your key audiences through a genuine two-way process, so that not only are they aware of what you are trying to achieve, but also you learn about their genuine concerns *and are ready to adjust your behaviour and decisions according to these concerns.*

This is a key point: it should not be looked at as taking away your right to manage your own business, but it should be looked at as responding and evolving according to the needs and desires of these major audiences who influence your organization and ultimately decide whether it thrives and survives.

When things aren't going well, public relations must become crisis management. But if a business goes into a crisis with a good reputation and solid relationships with its constituents and the media, the job is infinitely easier. A strong reputation is like an insurance policy: money in the bank for a rainy day. It probably won't help a firm avoid a nasty story in the newspaper, but it may keep it to a one-day story rather than the continued haemorrhaging in the media that can take a toll on a company's sales. Business experience and research have shown time and again that a good reputation helps a company sell its products, recruit the best and the brightest, and attract the most valuable business partners.

For the sceptics, the principle is absolutely fundamental: you only exist because people allow you to exist. If people do not want your organization to exist, then it will cease to be. When Gerald Ratner uttered his famous phrase about his own store's sherry decanter being 'total crap', people did not give his shops permission to exist any more. They voted with their feet and stayed away.

However, when Persil released a brand of washing powder that, it was later found, was destroying clothes, the brand had such a good reputation that people allowed it to continue to exist: they forgave it and wrote this off as a 'blip'. This is the power of 'stakeholders' (whom we will come to later on), and we are not just talking about customers. The media destroyed Ratner's reputation, but allowed Persil to 'get off lightly'. The message is that it is much better to work with your key players continually, to build up trust and a genuine understanding of their wants and desires.

Undertaking this fundamental shift in management policy could position your organization in the minds of your stakeholders as a socially responsible company, which is every bit as important as having a marketing strategy. Not only does it give you permission to exist, but it can be like gold dust in a public relations crisis. A survey by Business in the Community found that 86 per cent of people have a more positive image of a company when they can see evidence that the company is doing something to make the world a better place.

So what you need is a strategy that encourages mutual understanding and that is balanced: it is a genuine two-way communication in that what you tell your stakeholders affects what they think, say and write about you, and what they tell you affects the way you carry out your work. You will be influenced by each other and will each adjust your behaviour accordingly.

Your message

What is a message? It's a bit like saying, 'What is the sky?' We are all so familiar with it; there really is no need to explain it. But if you had been given the job of creating a better sky, you'd need to know a bit more about what you were dealing with. And so it is with communication – we need to look at what a message actually is before we can look at how to make better ones!

The whole purpose of communication is to get your message across to others. This is a process that involves both the sender of the message and the receiver. This process leaves room for error, with messages often misinterpreted by one or more of the parties involved. This causes unnecessary confusion and counter-productivity. In fact, a message is successful only when both the sender and the receiver perceive it in the same way.

By successfully getting your message across, you convey your thoughts and ideas effectively. When not successful, the thoughts and ideas that you convey do not necessarily reflect your own, causing a communications breakdown and creating roadblocks that stand in the way of your goals.

It might sound obvious, but getting your message across is of paramount importance in PR. To do this, you must understand what your message is, what audience you are sending it to and how it will be perceived.

Communication barriers can pop up at every stage of the communication process, which consists of *sender, message, channel, receiver, feedback* (see Figure 2.5).

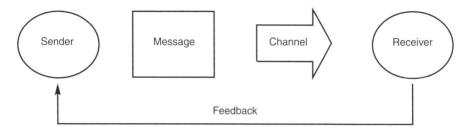

Figure 2.5 The communication process

All of these processes have the potential to create misunderstanding and confusion, so, to be an effective communicator and to get your point across without misunderstanding and confusion, your goal should be to lessen the frequency of these barriers at each stage of this process with clear, concise, accurate, well-planned communications. We follow the process through below:

● *Sender.* To establish yourself as an effective communicator, you must first establish credibility. In the business arena, this involves displaying knowledge of the subject, the audience and the context in which the message is delivered. You must also know your audience (individuals or groups to which you are delivering your message). Failure to understand who you are communicating to will result in delivering messages that are misunderstood.

● *Message.* Next, consider the message itself. Written, oral and non-verbal communications are affected by the sender's tone, method of organization, validity of the argument, what is communicated and what is left out, as well as the individual style of communicating. Messages also have intellectual and emotional components, with intellect allowing us the ability to reason and emotion allowing us to present motivational appeals, ultimately changing minds and actions.

● *Channel.* Messages are conveyed through channels, with 'verbal messages' including face-to-face meetings, interviews, telephone and videoconferencing, and 'written messages' including letters, press releases, e-mails, memos and reports.

● *Receiver.* These messages are delivered to an audience. No doubt you have in mind the actions or reactions you hope your message prompts from this audience. Keep in mind, though, that your audience also enters into the communication process with ideas and feelings that will undoubtedly influence their understanding of your message and their response. To be a successful communicator, you should consider these before delivering your message, acting appropriately.

● *Feedback.* Your audience will provide you with feedback, verbal and non-verbal reactions to your communicated message. Pay close attention to this feedback as it is crucial to ensuring that the audience understood your message.

Removing barriers at all these stages

To deliver your messages effectively, you must commit to breaking down the barriers that exist in each of these stages of the communication process.

Let's begin with the message itself. If your message is too lengthy or disorganized or contains errors, you can expect it to be misunderstood and misinterpreted. Use of poor verbal and body language can also confuse the message.

Barriers tend to stem from senders offering too much information too fast. When in doubt here, less is usually more. It's best to be mindful of the demands on other people's time, especially in today's ultra-busy society. Once you understand this, you need to work to understand your audience's culture, making sure you can converse and deliver your message to people of different backgrounds.

The importance of the feedback loop

The idea of a feedback loop is very important when delivering any message. This ensures that your messages have reached the right people and have been understood in the way you have intended.

Again, this has to be looked at properly. Simply recording what messages went out is an inadequate method. Even employing a measurement that shows to what extent people have understood a message's meaning and their impressions of it would still not be enough. It lacks the ability to measure behavioural and value change.

We need to work on a measurement that will indicate to what degree we are actually changing our key audience's opinions, behaviour and attitudes. Too often systems are established with effective outgoing material but ineffective confirmatory loops. In these cases two-way communication inevitably breaks down. This results in a lack of understanding, trust and most of all credibility. No communication is often better than wrong communication.

So our broad objectives in this area will be to create a two-way communication process with key audiences, which we will do by creating a comprehensive feedback system that you can genuinely react to, which will be addressed over the following sections of this book.

Who are your key audiences?

But who should these messages be going to? So far we've talked a lot about addressing your 'key audiences', 'target audiences' and 'stakeholders'. But just who are they? For a start, these terms are all interchangeable – we are always talking about the same groups of people. Different sets of people are affected by any one issue. From this perspective, there is no such thing as the 'general public'. Everyone is different and everything your business does affects different people in different ways. And similarly, what these people say and do affects what happens to your organization!

Going back to Grunig again, he lists four 'stakeholder categories', which are non-publics, latent publics, aware publics, and active publics:

- *Non-publics* have a low level of involvement with your organization and will not in all probability interact in any way with it.
- *Latent publics* include people who are unaware of their connections to your organization and what it does.
- *Aware publics* are those people who recognize they're somehow involved in or affected by an issue shared by others, but have not communicated about it to others.
- When they begin to communicate and organize to do something about the situation, they become *active publics*.

In today's world, the value of a company is measured not just by its balance sheet, but also by the strength of its relationships with those upon whom it is dependent for its success. It is the job of public relations to build and nurture those relationships with a company's stakeholders – investors, customers, partners and employees, to name just a few.

The importance of relationships and communications with stakeholders has grown as firms' net worth has increasingly come to depend on non-financial assets like corporate reputation, intellectual capital, public trust, employee commitment and brand loyalty. A recent study by the accounting firm Ernst & Young found that these intangible assets represent anywhere from 30 to 50 per cent of a company's market value!

Perhaps one of the most important attributes of a successful public relations programme is the ability to tune into the external world of an organization to discover issues and opportunities, and to identify friends and allies. In an age of intense media scrutiny and internet intrusiveness, virtually everything an organization does or says will find its way into the public domain.

Responding to those issues and critics will test your communications skills to the limit. It's never enough any more just to put out the company line and expect everyone to believe or act on it. Credibility is earned by an organization over time. And reputations are built by maintaining strong and lasting relationships and consistent communications with all of an organization's stakeholders.

The range of audiences and constituents for today's companies is broad – from customers to competitors, shareholders to MPs, employees to environmentalists. Because audiences' interests are rarely aligned and their motives are little understood, public relations strategies need to be able to deal with conflict and ambiguity.

Because some groups have particularly strong influences on others, PR strategies also need to understand the effects of audiences on each other. For example, employees make that all-important first impression on customers. That's why care must be taken to inform employees before announcing major decisions.

But while employees are stakeholders who have the strongest impact on a company's reputation, other audiences who have no stake in the company have the greatest credibility. The media, analysts and other third parties can be expected to be more objective and often more critical. Convincing sceptical third parties is the primary – and often the toughest – job of public relations.

According to the Chartered Institute of Public Relations, there are eight basic key stakeholder groups that need to be serviced:

1. the community at large or people living near or affected by the business's practices;

2. employees, managers and their unions;
3. customers – past, present and future;
4. suppliers of materials and non-financial services;
5. the money market, including shareholders, banks, insurers and investors;
6. distributors, agents, wholesalers and retailers;
7. potential employees, consultants and agents;
8. opinion leaders, particularly radio, television, press and other media professionals or activists, including lobbyists and pressure groups.

Stakeholder expectations

What do your stakeholders expect of you? What are their pains, concerns and desires that can be regarded as leverage points that can be used to get them to hear the messages that you need to communicate in order to meet your objectives?

To recap: firstly, you need to look at where you are starting from in terms of reputation, and then you need to establish in detail the audiences you need to reach. Secondly, you must consider the messages that you need to send them, how you want them to respond and when you need them to react.

You need to look at how you will select which channel through which to communicate to them. You need to look at costs, how feasible it is to manage the channel and whether it is sustainable over time. You then need to look at how you want your stakeholders to change: for example, creating values in favour of your organization in order actually to change the actions and behaviour of the stakeholders.

Because of your two-way interaction, you must not fall into the trap of deciding to tell them only what *you* think they should know: you need to let *them* ask the questions and not simply offer them messages that you think will please them.

How do you want the audiences to respond?

Ultimately the way you want your stakeholders to respond is, in effect, to become channels themselves through which to pass on your messages. The problem for any organization is that it is not feasible to engage with the entire population all of the time! What you need to look at is the targeting of your key stakeholders in a genuine two-way relationship in order for them not only to become positively predisposed to your values and thus less likely to form negative views, but also to pass on information to colleagues and the wider public. For example, journalists will choose relevant parts of messages and reframe them in language understandable to others and communicate them to other stakeholders.

Starting from the point that audiences will usually seek out the messages that they want – the messages that have the most gratifying content for them – we need to develop an active information campaign. Merely publishing information, for example, on a website for the press to access is not good enough. You need to actively help them locate the information that they want. This will be a key part of any PR strategy, as it will enable journalists to pass on the *right* information.

When do you need them to react?

The basis of this strategy is one built around developing relationships and trust. The difficulty is that educating stakeholders about values may take a long time, but although there is a long build-up there are also long-term effects. However, it is vital that you engage with them to see a palpable improvement in reputation.

This is why monitoring and evaluation are so important. It is useful to consider monitoring and evaluation as forms of control: a means by which we ensure that objectives are achieved. We need to constantly monitor the achievement of our objectives through a variety of ways, including involvement and observation, regular reporting, questioning and discussion, and records and routine statistics.

The quality of evaluation you undertake will be key when considering the complicated nature of improving relationships and stakeholders' perception of your reputation.

Agenda setting

When you've sorted out your message and your audience, this then gives you the unique ability to 'set the agenda' for what you want to be debated, a debate that, as an authority figure, you can lead! The term 'agenda setting' was first used in a study by Maxwell E McCombs and Donald L Shaw published in 1972. In the study, the researchers interviewed 100 undecided voters in Chapel Hill, North Carolina, and asked them what issues they were most concerned about in the coming (1968) election.

After determining the five issues the voters deemed most important, the researchers evaluated the media serving Chapel Hill (both print and broadcast) for the content of their stories. McCombs and Shaw found an almost perfect correlation between the types of stories that were covered most often and the voters' concern for the same issues.

McCombs and Shaw's research into agenda setting was not the first foray into the subject (although it was the first to coin the term), and it would not be the last. Several studies are done each year within the various disciplines of agenda-setting research. Generally, the studies seem mostly to confirm that agenda setting does in fact take place and that media attention towards stories is the most important factor involved in shaping the public's view of the stories' relative importance. In fact, studies have shown that the mere number of times a story is repeated in the news will affect people's perception of the story's importance, regardless of what is said about the topic.

This is why PR is so important – it gives *you* this vital ability to set the agenda, thus fundamentally affecting people's views. There are three types of agenda: the media agenda (print and broadcast), the public agenda (what the 'word on the street' is) and the policy agenda (usually to do with government policies). Each one tends to affect the others, but the media agenda undoubtedly wields the most power when trying to drum up a debate.

But if you think PR is just about agenda setting by getting stories in the media, then, I'm afraid, you'll have to think again, and this is due in no small part to the US presidential election of 1940. This is when the academics Lazarsfeld, Berelson and Gaudet conducted the first full-scale investigation of the effects of political mass communication.

Their research was originally based on the simplistic 'hypodermic needle' model of media influence, where it was assumed that a message would be transmitted from the mass media to a 'mass audience', who would absorb the message as an arm would absorb whatever was pumped into it by a hypodermic needle. However, their investigations suggested that media effects were minimal and that the idea of a 'mass audience' was inadequate and misguided because social influences had a major effect on the process of opinion formation and sharply limited the media's effect.

The study concluded that only 5 per cent of people changed their voting behaviour as a result of media messages! Their exposure to election broadcasts turned out to be a relatively poor predictor of their voting behaviour, particularly when compared with other factors such as their communication with friends, union members, business colleagues and the political tradition they had grown up in. This view of media effects was confirmed in a variety of other investigations and came to be known as the 'limited effects paradigm' of media influence.

Consequently Lazarsfeld and his colleagues developed the notion of a 'two-step' flow of media messages, a process in which opinion leaders played a vitally important role. Basically, the findings showed that:

- our responses to media messages will be *mediated through our social relationships*, the effects of media messages being sharply limited by interpersonal relationships and the formal or social groups that we mix with;
- it is misleading to think of receivers as members of a 'mass audience' since that implies that they are all equal in their reception of media messages, whereas in fact *some play a more active role than others*;
- receiving a message does not imply responding to it;
- there are some people among the media audience who act as *opinion leaders* – typically such people use the mass media more than the average, mix more than the average across social classes and see themselves and are seen by others as having an influence on others.

No 'opinion leader' is an opinion leader in all aspects of life. For example, the car mechanic in your local pub may not use the media much at all because he's always working late. Nevertheless, he knows a lot about cars and so what the rest of those in the pub 'know' from the media about different makes of car will be influenced by his views.

We also can't suggest that people are either active opinion leaders or passive followers of opinion leaders. Apart from the evidence that people can be opinion leaders on some matters and not on others, there is also the objection that some people may be neither leaders nor followers, but quite simply detached from much media output.

Much depends also on the accessibility of countervailing opinions. In the 1940s the general public would have had access to far fewer sources of information than they have today and may, broadly speaking, have had less time to access those sources. Under such circumstances it is likely that an opinion leader in the community will be especially influential.

This was recognized by the Nazi Party in its gradual rise to power during the 1920s and 1930s. Nazi agitation and propaganda became increasingly successful at forcing themselves on to the front pages of newspapers, thus becoming an everyday topic of conversation. The Nazis were particularly keen to capitalize on that attention, directing it in their preferred direction through influencing the leading members of the various small associations that were spread throughout German communities.

Where local leaders enjoying respectability and influence were won over, further converts often rapidly followed. In the relatively homogeneous villages in Schleswig-Holstein, where feelings about the 'Weimar system' were running high on account of the agrarian crisis, the push from one or two farmers' leaders could result in a local landslide to the Nazi Party.

You should never underestimate the importance of gaining credible, heavyweight endorsement from opinion leaders and getting them to add their weight to media agenda setting. Only when you have completed this circle can you claim to have had a successful PR campaign.

Campaigns

When you start putting together a PR strategy, you will come to the point where you need to begin instigating a campaign. Although this sounds fairly straightforward, there is a theory behind it that is important. The main four characteristics of a campaign are that it:

1. has specific results;
2. is aimed at large audiences;
3. has a given time period;
4. is an organized set of communication activities.

It will usually involve a number of subtle techniques over and above agenda setting, which we have already explored. It will also feature the idea of *framing*, which is concerned with how the organization and packaging of information (in the media, for example) affect people's perceptions of that information. Many campaigns are grounded in this theory and therefore attempt to affect how the public thinks about an issue by changing the way that the media frame it.

Priming is the process in which the media attend to some issues and not others and thereby alter the standards by which people evaluate issues, people or objects. For example, the more the media pay attention to the issue of campaign finance reform in an election, the more the public will use that issue to evaluate the candidates. This theory is based on the assumption that people do not have elaborate knowledge about a lot of things (especially about politics) and do not take into account all of what they do know when making decisions. Rather they make decisions based on what comes to mind first.

Effective campaigns

To succeed, a campaign must have:

- realistic goals;
- a mixture of mass and interpersonal communication;
- a recognition of different target audiences.

Table 2.1 illustrates the needs of an effective campaign.

Table 2.1 Needs of an effective campaign

Tasks	Issues to consider
1. To capture the attention of the right audience.	Defining the target audience, selecting channels to reach the audience, attracting sufficient attention.
2. To deliver an understandable and credible message.	Source credibility, message clarity, fit with prior knowledge, duration of exposure.
3. To deliver a message that influences the beliefs or understanding of the audience.	Provide information, direct attention, trigger norms, change underlying values and preferences.
4. To create social contexts that lead towards desired outcomes.	Understand the pressures that govern the behaviour of interest.

Models of how a campaign is supposed to work ultimately drive the selection of outcomes that get measured. There is often more to an evaluation than assessing the usual outcome suspects: knowledge, attitudes and behaviours.

When we measure the direct outputs of campaigns we call this *process evaluation*. This is a 'measure of effort' – what and how much the campaign accomplished and its distribution and reach. While process measures may not tell much about the campaign's effects, they can help determine *why* a campaign did or did not work. These methods are mostly concerned with measuring the reach of the campaign. They have the challenge of tracking outcomes in the diverse communication technologies of print, radio, television and the internet.

Outcome evaluations are 'measures of effect' that come about in the target audiences as a result of the campaign. This focuses on the attitudes that most campaigns try to change. Methods most often used to assess campaign outcomes include surveys or polling.

Impact evaluations are measures of the ultimate aggregate results of a campaign's outcomes. They track progress towards the campaign's goals or desired results and, if the campaign is trying to change behaviour in a sizeable number of individuals, then this assesses the long-term outcomes of these changes. A 'designated driver' campaign to reduce traffic fatalities due to drink driving would be a good example. Assessing impact usually requires experimental research design as it needs to be heavily tailored to the individual campaign.

Conclusion

The most important finding from a major survey of 850 US and European opinion leaders is that opinion leaders are eight times more likely to believe information that they get from articles or news coverage than information in corporate or product advertising. This may not be surprising to public relations practitioners, but it does make us wonder why so many corporations, particularly those facing serious credibility issues, still spend an inordinately high percentage of their resources on advertising.

Building successful companies and brands isn't about selling. It's about building trust and understanding through open, interactive and information-rich relationships. That's the domain of public relations – and that's the challenge and opportunity for the small business.

The more people perceive companies as foreign or global, the less they trust them. In fact, the fall-off in trust among opinion leaders, in both the United States and Europe, is dramatic – more than 40 per cent.

Just as people tend to trust the companies they work for more than any other, people have a natural affinity towards companies they perceive to be part of the local community and culture. For a global brand to succeed in a foreign market, it must build strong relationships with as many local constituencies as possible and adopt a communications policy and style that fit the market. Messages are easily distorted, particularly after they go through language, cultural and media filters, so it's important that communications flow from local operations and agents rather than from distant corporate headquarters.

Trust in certain US brands is significantly lower in Europe than in the Unites States. For example, McDonald's is trusted by 55 per cent of the responders in the United Sates but only by 22 per cent in Europe. Similarly, Coca-Cola enjoyed a 66 per cent trust rating in the United States, but dropped to 37 per cent in Europe. Bottom line: it's increasingly difficult to be warmly accepted in the global community unless you are an active, integral part of it, giving small local businesses a massive advantage over their global counterparts.

We all agree on the value of a good corporate reputation. It plays a large role in everyone's opinion of a company's products and services and makes them more willing to pay a premium for its products and services.

As already stated, opinion leaders are eight times more likely to believe news stories and articles than information conveyed through corporate advertising. Furthermore, there is no single most popular source of credible information that people turn to for news and information. Articles in newspapers, news weeklies and business magazines and radio and TV news coverage all carry an implied level of credibility that readers and viewers appreciate.

Companies cannot buy credibility. To move from a 'buy it' to a 'be it' approach, businesses must help build conversations with people who are respected. Advertising can reinforce brands and reputations *after* their credibility has been established.

We trust more slowly because media and information inundate us, leaving us with what is called 'continuous partial attention'. We don't give our full attention easily or quickly. Rather, we commit it gradually. As a result, companies and brands must continually earn trust by using media and independent experts, by communicating with audiences when and how they want, and by using multiple communications channels that offer flexible formats for information exchange.

This means that companies need to find meaningful connections between the business and its products and services, and must keep the company's reputation consistent. More importantly, businesses must engage an array of stakeholders – consumers, regulators, legislators, media, analysts, academics and so on – and build solid relationships with them. Business today is everybody's business, and the firms that develop open, interactive and information-rich relationships with each of these influencer groups will win.

Case study

Background

Toy and model vehicle manufacture Corgi's Definitive Bond Collection marked the introduction of the most comprehensive range of iconic James Bond 007 movie vehicles. A total of 11 vehicles – from Bond's Aston Martin DB5 in *Goldfinger* to the state-of-the-art BMW Z8 in *The World Is Not Enough* – composed the new collection.

The Red Brick team believed that a relationship-building event would be the most effective way of communicating the Corgi brand proposition, as well as building strong relationships with a section of the media that had proven difficult to target. The strength of conviction was such that Red Brick offset the cost of time against this project with income generated from mark-up on bought-in costs. It was anticipated that the initial investment of time would reap great returns for Corgi, while providing the collateral for Red Brick to renegotiate an annual fee at a higher level to accommodate future relationship-building events.

Objectives

Red Brick's brief was to target a wider audience for Corgi Classics, the UK's leading brand of die-cast model vehicles for the adult collector, using the new Bond range to create maximum awareness for a minimum cost, achieving the following core objectives:

- Raise awareness of Corgi Classics and broaden appeal among a new and largely untapped audience.
- Build relationships with the key consumer media (men's, women's style, film, weekend supplements, national and broadcast).

- Create interest in the range from the onset of product availability and support sales activity.

Plan and strategy

Red Brick's strategy utilized a series of cost-effective and creative tactics:

- Stage a launch event at a select London venue located conveniently for the core target media – relationship building on a one-to-one basis.
- Create a James Bond-themed event – generate interest and maximize attendance.
- Develop a special, one-off press gift drawing on the collecting idiom of limited edition models – sustain interest.

Target audience

- Men's and women's style press.
- Film and entertainment press.
- Automobile/vehicle media.
- National weekend supplements.
- Nationals.
- Broadcast.

Key advocacy

- Corgi's green light for event.
- Buy-in to event by 'wish list' of target vertical press.
- Production of collectable film canister press gift.
- Negotiation of free BMW Z8 for use at the venue.
- Presence of Oddjob and Jaws Bond movie character lookalikes at venue.
- Stylized Bond theme in venue.

Execution and implementation

Working to a structured timetable to meet lead-times and budget restrictions, Red Brick's main actions included:

- venue and timing research;
- sourcing caterers, florists, props and music;
- defining target press list, particularly freelancers;
- producing personalized invitations with 'secret' admission password, plus miniature bottle of Martini 'shaken, not stirred';
- designing and producing a movie-themed press gift comprising original cellulose film canisters with digitally printed insert detailing the limited-edition nature of this special commemorative pack with models;

- negotiating with BMW's head office for free loan of a BMW Z8 (worth £80,000-plus and one of only a handful in the UK) for show outside the event venue;
- booking Oddjob and Jaws lookalikes to attend the launch and pose with each journalist for a photograph that was sent as a post-event thank-you;
- locating a James Bond film set on which to stage all models (including resin prototypes of pre-production models) for press to view.

A press pack was provided to all journalists attending and mailed to secondary consumer media post-event. Remaining film canisters were offered to key titles to use for competitions to maximize return on expenditure.

Results and evaluation

From a total of 40 invitees, 22 selected press contacts attended the event including *Vanity Fair*, *GQ*, *Arena*, the *Daily Express*, the *Daily Telegraph*, the *Funday Times*, the *Daily Star*, Hoot! website and cable channel *Movie News*. The collector and automotive press were also well represented with coverage achieved in major titles across all the target sectors.

Forty press cuttings were recorded, representing a total circulation of 7,236,494 and an advertising rate card equivalent of £28,209 – a hefty return on the initial cost budget investment of £7,500.

Corgi's marketing director Angus MacLeod said: 'It was a minimal budget very well spent. We reached a good cross-section of heavyweight consumer and horizontal press with immediate high-profile coverage following the event, which has continued over a considerable period of time. The high visibility created for the brand through the event has had a positive impact on sales with demand exceeding our initial expectations threefold.'

The event also had a major impact on the broader Corgi PR campaign. The development of close relationships with the key vertical press has generated continued presence of Corgi in this press. Coverage since the event has reached a circulation of 6.4 million, with a £21,500 advertising value equivalent.

3 Environmental analysis

Introduction

Here we will look at the idea of 'environmental analysis': we will guide your business through conducting PEST (political, environmental, social, technological) and SWOT (strengths, weaknesses, opportunities, threats) analyses by suggesting as many areas in which to find information as possible. The difference with this analysis, however, is that when looking at opportunities it will take into account points identified in the PEST analysis. This means that opportunities will be identified that can be taken advantage of in your business's current environment, and we will show you how. This chapter will give you tangible business objectives, the importance of which will also be illustrated.

Environmental analysis

We need to analyse the situation that your firm is in and the factors that affect it. These are both internal factors such as history, policy, procedures and employee attitudes, and external factors such as political and economic trends, and technological and environmental issues.

A good way to analyse these is through: 1) PEST analysis; and 2) SWOT analysis. A PEST analysis looks at the key external trends and drivers of change outside the control of your business and weighs up their potential to affect the firm. A SWOT analysis then identifies which of these issues the business needs to deal with, and can then develop a strategy detailing future plans. We'll now look at both of these in a bit more detail.

What is a PEST analysis?

A PEST analysis (also sometimes called STEP, STEEP or PESTLE analysis) looks at the external business environment. In fact, it would be better to call this kind of analysis a *business environmental analysis* but the acronym PEST is easy to remember and so has stuck. It is very important that a business considers its environment before beginning the PR process. In fact, environmental analysis should be continuous and feed all aspects of planning. The analysis examines the impact of each of these factors (and their interplay with each other) on the business. The results can then be used to take advantage of opportunities and to make contingency plans for threats when preparing business and strategic plans.

You need to consider each PEST factor, as they all play a part in determining your overall business environment. Thus, when looking at political factors you should consider the impact of any political or legislative changes that could affect your business. If you are operating in more than one country then you will need to look at each country in turn. Political factors include aspects such as laws on maternity rights, data protection and even environmental policy: these three examples alone have an impact on employment terms, information access, product specification and business processes in many businesses globally.

Obviously politicians don't operate in a vacuum, and many political changes result from changes in the economy or in social and cultural values, for example. And although tax rates are generally decided by politicians, tax decisions generally also include economic considerations such as what the state of the economy is. In Europe, the politicians drove the introduction of the euro currency, but the impacts include economic factors: cross-border pricing, European interest rates, bank charges, price transparency and so on. Other economic factors include exchange rates, inflation levels, income growth, debt and savings levels (which impact available money) and consumer and business confidence. There can also be narrow industry measures that become important. Issues such as the availability of skilled labour or raw-material costs can impact industries in different ways.

Advances in technology can have a major impact on business success, with companies that fail to keep up often going out of business. Technological change also affects political and economic aspects, and plays a part in how people view their world. Just as one example, the internet has had a major influence on the ways consumers and businesses research and purchase products. Whereas 10 or even 5 years ago it was rare for consumers to consider cross-border purchases, this is now becoming common via services such as eBay, with the result that even small businesses can now serve a global market.

Politicians are still coming to grips with the tax issues involved. Meanwhile the music industry has still not found an effective solution to the threat posed by the successors to Napster. Environmental factors to consider here include the impact of climate change: water and winter fuel costs could change dramatically if the world warms by only a couple of degrees.

Ultimately, however, all the various PEST factors are governed by 'sociocultural' factors. These are the elements that build society. Social factors influence people's choices and include societal beliefs, values and attitudes. So understanding changes in this area can be crucial, as they lead to political and societal change. You need to consider demographic changes and also consumer views on your product and industry sector; environmental issues (especially if your product involves hazardous or potentially damaging production processes); lifestyle changes and attitudes to health, wealth, age (children, the elderly, etc), gender, work and leisure. Added complications when looking at social and cultural factors are differences in ethnic and social groups. Not all groups have the same attitudes, and this influences how they view various products and services.

Your business's PR environment is made up of:

1. the internal environment, eg staff (or internal customers), office technology, wages and finance, etc;
2. the micro-environment, eg your external customers, agents and distributors, suppliers, competitors, etc;
3. the macro-environment, eg political (and legal) forces, economic forces, sociocultural forces and technological forces: these are known as PEST factors.

The PEST analysis is a useful tool for understanding market growth or decline, and so the position, potential and direction for a business. A PEST analysis is a business measurement tool and uses headings that are a framework for reviewing a situation and can also, like SWOT analysis (which we will cover below), be used to review a strategy or position, direction of a company, a marketing proposition, or idea. As PEST factors are essentially external, completing a PEST analysis is helpful prior to completing a SWOT analysis (a SWOT analysis – strengths, weaknesses, opportunities, threats – is based broadly on half internal and half external factors). A PEST analysis measures a market; a SWOT analysis measures a business unit, proposition or idea.

The PEST model is sometimes extended (some would say unnecessarily) to seven factors, by adding ecological, legislative and industry analysis (the model is then known as PESTELI). However, if completed properly, the basic PEST analysis should naturally cover these 'additional' factors: ecological factors are found under the four main PEST headings; legislative factors would normally be covered under the political heading; and industry analysis is effectively covered under the economic heading.

A SWOT analysis measures a business unit or proposition; a PEST analysis measures the market potential and situation, particularly indicating growth or decline, and thereby market attractiveness, business potential and suitability of access – market potential and 'fit', in other words. PEST analysis uses four perspectives, which give a logical structure, in this case organized by the PEST format, that helps understanding, presentation, discussion and decision making. The four dimensions are an extension of a basic two-heading list of pros and cons.

PEST analysis can be used for PR and business development assessment and decision making, and the PEST template encourages proactive thinking, rather than relying on habitual or instinctive reactions. As with SWOT analysis, it is important to identify clearly the subject of a PEST analysis, because a PEST analysis is a four-way perspective in relation to a particular business unit or proposition – if you blur the focus you will produce a blurred picture – so be clear about the market that you use PEST to analyse.

What areas you need to cover

When developing a PEST analysis we need to ask what external factors are affecting the business, how these are affecting it, which are currently the most important factors and which will be the most important over the next few years. The areas in which you need to gather information will include:

- *Political:*
  - ecological/environmental issues;
  - current legislation in the home market;
  - future legislation;
  - European/international legislation;
  - regulatory bodies and processes;
  - government policies;
  - government term and change;
  - trading policies;
  - funding, grants and initiatives;
  - home market lobbying and pressure groups;
  - international pressure groups.
- *Economic:*
  - home economy situation;
  - home economy trends;
  - overseas economies and trends;
  - general taxation issues;
  - taxation specific to products and services;
  - seasonality and weather issues;
  - market and trade cycles;
  - specific industry factors;
  - market routes and distribution trends;
  - customer and end-user drivers;
  - interest and exchange rates.
- *Social:*
  - lifestyle trends;
  - demographics;
  - consumer attitudes and opinions;
  - media views;
  - law changes affecting social factors;
  - brand, company and technology image;
  - consumer buying patterns;
  - fashion and role models;
  - major events and influences;
  - buying access and trends;
  - ethnic and religious factors;
  - advertising and publicity.
- *Technological:*
  - competing technology development;
  - research funding;

- – associated and dependent technologies;
- – replacement technology and solutions;
- – maturity of technology;
- – manufacturing maturity and capacity;
- – information and communications;
- – consumer buying mechanisms and technology;
- – technology legislation;
- – innovation potential;
- – technology access, licensing and patents;
- – intellectual property issues.

When you begin a PEST analysis, you need to take some practical steps to research your environment. The types of things you should be doing when conducting a PEST analysis are:

- *Media coverage:* investigating reports in newspapers, television, radio, books and magazines to garner recorded opinion about the firm's industrial sector from analysts, interest groups, competitors, politicians and other opinion formers.
- *Internet monitoring:* tapping into internet discussion areas, chat-rooms and other websites to see what people are saying about the firm's industrial sector.
- *Tracking the political situation:* looking at any recent political developments that involve the firm's industrial sector, and searching through agendas and minutes of government meetings.
- *The grapevine:* gathering feedback and intelligence from people within the firm's industrial sector, and talking and listening to other key people within the industry.

Example

Trevor's Terrific Travel Ltd is a small travel agency based in Anytown. They have a successful business, so much so that they are getting ready to take over another small travel agency on the other side of town. They are using this opportunity to take stock of their business and the industry it operates in so that they can see what can be improved and what areas they need to focus on to generate more income.

Trevor's Terrific Travel Ltd produces the following PEST analysis to look at what external factors are affecting the two businesses (themselves and their new acquisition), which are currently the most important factors and which will be the most important over the next few years:

- *Political:*
    - Tourism across the world has been reeling from the impact of the US terror attacks.
    - US airlines have announced plans to shed more than 100,000 jobs in the wake of the attacks, as a result of a sharp slump in business.
    - Government influences tourism through fiscal and regulatory policy and through funding of statutory bodies: British Tourist Authority, area tourist boards, enterprise networks, local authorities and other national agencies (eg forestry, the built and natural environment, arts and sport).
    - There is a current skills shortage in the industry and a decrease in the selection of tourism and hospitality as a career choice, which government should address.
    - As for the tax and regulatory regime, the VAT rate (set by government) specifically puts the UK at a competitive disadvantage with other European destinations.
- *Economic:*
    - Tourism nationally has continued to expand.
    - Spending by overnight tourists in the 1990s has continued to increase although at a slower rate than in the previous decade, eg 30 per cent increase in domestic overnight tourism, 80 per cent in overseas tourism.
    - There was considerable growth in the number of overseas visitors from 1987 to 1997 (average 5 per cent annual growth in international tourism trips).
    - Since 1997 growth has slowed and in 1999 overseas visitor numbers to Britain fell by 1 per cent.
    - The domestic market has grown much more slowly over the same period (average annual growth of 1.5 per cent in domestic tourism trips).
- *Sociocultural:*
    - Slow domestic market growth is largely due to the continued decline in long holidays.
    - In contrast, the market for domestic short breaks, additional holidays and VFR (visiting friends and relatives) has shown consistent growth.

- Short holidays of one to three nights now account for 25 per cent of tourism trips in England. This has been the fastest-growing segment in recent years, and this trend is likely to continue.
- A significant majority of short breaks are taken in serviced accommodation, including hotels and B&Bs.
- There is a bias towards higher socio-economic groups (ABs), and the types of holidays that the company sells are popular with both young adults and active retired people.
- Business tourism remains important but fluctuates with the strength of the economy. There was a 10 per cent increase in domestic business trips over the period 1994–98.
- The vast proportion of leisure day visits continues to be eating and drinking out (18 per cent), visiting friends and relatives (17 per cent), walking (15 per cent) and shopping (12 per cent).
- Visits to attractions represent less than 10 per cent of all day trips and in 1998, for the first time since 1991, there was a decrease in the number of visits to a constant sample of attractions and, for the first time, there were more closures than new openings of attractions.

- *Technological:*
  - The developments in information communication technologies (ICTs) and the internet in particular have revolutionized the entire tourism industry, generating new business models, changing the structure of the tourism distribution channels and re-engineering all processes.
  - Tourism suppliers, destinations and stakeholders have all been influenced.
  - E-tourism is bringing together some of the most rapidly developing industries including information communications technologies, tourism/travel/hospitality and strategic management/marketing/planning.
  - In the electronic marketplace, e-businesses dealing with e-consumers, e-government, e-partners and other e-businesses on an e-platform are being facilitated by the radically evolving ICTs.

Going back to the areas you should cover, and using the example above, write down issues for your own business. Use the margins or additional sheets of paper or the back of a beer mat if you think of more than four:

- *Political:*

  _____

  _____

  _____

  _____

- *Economic:*

  _____

  _____

  _____

  _____

- *Sociocultural:*

  _____

  _____

  _____

  _____

- *Technological:*

  _____

  _____

  _____

  _____

Good job! Here is where most people would now put the PEST analysis to one side, happy that they have at least 'thought about' these kinds of issues. But this is not good enough for us! We now need to whittle down the more important issues. This is where we go back to Trevor's Terrific Travel Ltd who have gone back through their PEST analysis and picked out their top two areas under each heading:

- *Political:*
  - Tourism across the world has been reeling from the impact of the US terror attacks.
  - There is a current skill shortage in the industry and a decrease in the selection of tourism and hospitality as a career choice, which government should address.
- *Economic:*
  - Tourism nationally has continued to expand.
  - Spending by overnight tourists in the 1990s has continued to increase although at a slower rate than in the previous decade, eg 30 per cent increase in domestic overnight tourism, 80 per cent in overseas tourism.
- *Sociocultural:*
  - There is a bias towards higher socio-economic groups (ABs), and the types of holidays that the company sells are popular with both young adults and active retired people.
  - Business tourism remains important but fluctuates with the strength of the economy.
- *Technological:*
  - Tourism suppliers, destinations and stakeholders have all been influenced.
  - The developments in information communication technologies (ICTs) and the internet in particular have revolutionized the entire tourism industry.

You now need to make similar decisions – out of all the things you have listed, decide what you think are the top two biggest issues in each category:

- *Political:*

  _____

  _____

- *Economic:*

  _____

  _____

- *Sociocultural:*

- *Technological:*

Case study

Background

The Science Museum took a major risk. They brought in Grossology – an exhibition dealing with farts, snot, poo and other 'nasties' not discussed in polite society. This seemingly light-hearted children's exhibition was one of the most challenging propositions in the Science Museum's history, because:

- The museum is a national institution, for which many people feel a sense of ownership; some would think Grossology was not 'right' for the museum.
- Grossology is a US import – and uses US technology.
- It has an entry charge and clearly targets children.
- The exhibition's accessible treatment of science could provoke charges that the museum was 'dumbing down'. They had recently been accused of this, with stories in the *Observer* and other papers wrongly asserting that the museum was to replace galleries with burger bars and coffee shops.
- The marketplace had become increasingly crowded and competitive, as the major free museums and galleries (as well as other attractions) competed for visitors to paid-for exhibitions – which provide vital sources of funds.

The Science Museum therefore elected to be bolder, more strategic and more daring – to rip up their own rule book and treat Grossology as though it was their first-ever exhibition. The attitude was particularly important as they were working on an extremely tight budget.

Ultimately the campaign exceeded all expectations. Grossology was lauded by media as diverse as the *Beano* and Radio 4's *Today* programme. It delivered the visitor numbers and income required and, above all, enhanced the overall reputation of a 100-year-old institution. Rather than become a lightning rod for conservative criticism, the exhibition became an emblem for a bolder, more adventurous museum. It even earned four minutes on *Have I Got News for You?*

and the approval of *The Times* leader, which congratulated the museum for 'boldly going where no sane biology master has gone before'.

Objectives

- To further the Science Museum's agenda of reaching and engaging new audiences.
- To surprise, amuse and intrigue audiences and help shift outdated perceptions about the museum.
- To generate 995 paying visitors a day during May and 1,076 a day in June and July, with additional increases during school holidays from the target audience – children aged 6–14 and their parents.

Execution and implementation

Pre-launch

Early planning focused on three campaign tasks:

- to change the way the museum traditionally prepared for exhibition launches;
- to use a wider range of media more creatively, to create sustained publicity;
- to recruit 'opinion formers' to help address certain audiences.

The creative approach was to present the exhibition as great fun and truly disgusting to children, and fun but backed by solid science to parents.
   Activities included:

- Securing the endorsement of authoritative health education bodies (eg Royal Institute of Public Health) to build credibility.
- Securing participation of the *Beano* as a unique communication channel, loved by children, trusted by parents and warmly regarded by the media. Liaising directly with the editor, the Science Museum succeeded in working the exhibition into a regular feature, thereby establishing their 'right' to talk to kids. This was a first for them *and* the comic.
- Preview for long-lead media using early availability of media information and a video walk-through of Grossology.
- Intensive training of staff (including preparation of written support material and staging 'grossness' workshops) to ensure appropriate responses to issues including:
  - dumbing down;
  - use of US technology in the exhibition;
  - real science content.

- Media training of Science Museum spokespeople, who were then selected to fit different media, eg Head of Science Museum (strong educational background) fielded to combat charge of 'dumbing down'; 23-year-old front-of-house staff member (a Grossologist, of course!) used to appear on children's programmes.
- Special attention given to securing listings press through early information and competitions.
- Long-term initiatives launched.

Launch

- *Beano* feature given to all media invited to the press preview.
- Press preview the day before opening – 60 attendees including all national broadsheets, TV, BBC Radio 4 and children's publications.
- School children invited for photocall and tours of the exhibition led by museum staff.
- Substantial coverage, with pictures, in *The Times*, *Daily Telegraph*, *Independent*, *Daily Express* and BBC *News*, plus Radio 4's *Today* programme, 5 Live and many others.
- Sell-out attendances.

During the lifetime of the exhibition

- A website survey into 'gross' habits built background noise as the exhibition opened, generating 4,500 entries. Results spearheaded their summer holiday push, with coverage in the media as diverse as *The Times* (the front page – a first for the museum) and page three of the *Sun*.
- A viral campaign launched to direct visitors to the Grossology website – 3,300 people e-mailed with a melodic computer fart-organ, which could then be e-mailed on.
- Constant dialogue with London guides, 'best days out' pages, children's media and parenting publications to maintain presence over the lifetime of the exhibition.
- A major push with regional newspapers in south-east England built profile and increased holiday traffic. It featured an article written by the Head of the Science Museum, a set of foul facts and promotional vouchers. It ran in 120 titles.
- Grossology hosted an attempt to break the world record for the loudest burp, which was covered live by Channel 4's *RI:SE* and Sky News, plus ITV *London Today*.
- The museum took its show on the road – reaching out to wider audiences with a staging of a specially created show that ran in Covent Garden Market for two weeks, another first for the museum.

Evaluation and measurement

Results:

- The most substantial and positive media coverage ever obtained for an exhibition at the Science Museum – with the museum being applauded for its ambition in staging Grossology.
- Unprecedented breadth of coverage from the *Beano* to BBC Radio 4's *Today*, the *Daily Telegraph*, *Newsround* and *Have I Got News for You?* – achieving the museum's objective of balancing fun with science, and communicating a more modern, accessible impression of the museum.
- Reached much wider and more diverse audiences than usual, eg children through TV, comics, the *Funday Times*, etc and wider socio-economic groups through inner London weekly newspapers, the *Sun*, London radio, etc.
- It was estimated that there were around 70 million opportunities to see Grossology through PR.
- No negative media comment – all negative questions were disarmed by spokespeople.
- Grossology reached media way beyond the scope of an exhibition launch, such as *The Times* leader column and *Have I Got News for You?*
- Launch weekend sold out – 3,814 visitors, nearly double the target.
- Excellent figures during half-terms with 2,527 visitors on one day alone, two and a half times the target.
- Research among visitors shows that media coverage was the primary driver of traffic to the exhibition.
- Grossology was one of the factors behind the museum winning both the London Tourist Board and the English Tourism Council visitor attraction of the year awards.

The SWOT analysis

Put the PEST analysis to one side for the moment; we'll come back to it soon. PEST is useful before SWOT – not generally vice versa – and PEST definitely helps to identify SWOT factors. There is overlap between PEST and SWOT, in that similar factors will appear in each. That said, PEST and SWOT certainly give two different perspectives: 1) PEST assesses a market, including competitors, from the standpoint of a particular proposition or a business. 2) SWOT is an assessment of a business or a proposition, whether your own or a competitor's.

The four headings in PEST vary in significance depending on the type of business, for example social factors are more obviously relevant to consumer businesses or a B2B business close to the consumer end of the supply chain, whereas political factors are more obviously relevant to a global munitions supplier or aerosol propellant manufacturer.

But a SWOT analysis is a tool for all businesses that need to audit their environment. It is the stage of planning that helps PR to focus on key issues. Once key issues have been identified, they feed into PR objectives. Here we are using it in conjunction with a PEST analysis for audit and analysis. It is a very popular tool for PR as it is quick and easy to learn.

Completing a SWOT

SWOT analysis is not just another academic gimmick, but something that has been painfully refined over many years. Just to remind you, SWOT stands for strengths, weaknesses, opportunities and threats. Two of these are known as 'internal factors' and the other two are known as 'external factors'.

Strengths and weaknesses are *internal* factors. A *strength* could be:

- your specialist marketing expertise;
- a new, innovative product or service;
- location of your business;
- quality processes and procedures;
- any other aspect of your business that adds value to your product or service.

A *weakness* could be:

- lack of marketing expertise;
- undifferentiated products and services (ie in relation to your competitors);
- location of your business;
- poor-quality goods or services;
- damaged reputation.

Opportunities and threats are *external* factors. An *opportunity* could be:

- a developing market tool such as the internet;
- mergers, joint ventures or strategic alliances;
- moving into new market segments that offer improved profits;
- a new international market;
- a market vacated by an ineffective competitor.

A *threat* could be:

- a new competitor in your home market;
- price wars with competitors;
- a competitor with a new, innovative product or service;
- competitors with superior access to channels of distribution;
- taxation being introduced on your product or service.

Simple rules for successful SWOT analysis:

- Be realistic about the strengths and weaknesses of your organization.
- Analysis should distinguish between where your organization is today and where it could be in the future.
- Be specific. Avoid grey areas.
- Always analyse in the context of your competition, ie better than or worse than your competition.
- Keep your SWOT short and simple. Avoid complexity and over-analysis.
- SWOT is subjective.

Below are sample questions for you to answer. They are examples, or discussion points, for you to think about when you come to do your own SWOT analysis:

- *Strengths:*
  - Advantages of proposition?
  - Capabilities?
  - Competitive advantages?
  - USPs (unique selling points)?
  - Resources, assets, people?
  - Experience, knowledge, data?
  - Financial reserves, likely returns?

- Marketing: reach, distribution, awareness?
- Innovative aspects?
- Location and geographical?
- Price, value, quality?
- Accreditations, qualifications, certifications?
- Processes, systems, IT, communications?
- Cultural, attitudinal, behavioural?
- Management cover, succession?

- *Weaknesses:*
  - Disadvantages of proposition?
  - Gaps in capabilities?
  - Lack of competitive strength?
  - Reputation, presence and reach?
  - Financials?
  - Own known vulnerabilities?
  - Timescales, deadlines and pressures?
  - Cash flow, start-up cash-drain?
  - Continuity, supply chain robustness?
  - Effects on core activities, distraction?
  - Reliability of data, plan predictability?
  - Morale, commitment, leadership?
  - Accreditations, etc?
  - Processes and systems, etc?
  - Management cover, succession?

- *Opportunities:*
  - Market developments?
  - Competitors' vulnerabilities?
  - Industry or lifestyle trends?
  - Technology development and innovation?
  - Global influences?
  - New markets, vertical, horizontal?
  - Niche target markets?
  - Geographical, export, import?
  - New USPs?
  - Tactics: surprise, major contracts, etc?
  - Business and product development?
  - Information and research?
  - Partnerships, agencies, distribution?
  - Volumes, production, economies?
  - Seasonal, weather, fashion influences?

- *Threats:*
  - Political effects?
  - Legislative effects?
  - Environmental effects?
  - IT developments?
  - Competitor intentions: various?
  - Market demand?
  - New technologies, services, ideas?
  - Vital contracts and partners?
  - Sustaining internal capabilities?
  - Obstacles faced?
  - Insurmountable weaknesses?
  - Loss of key staff?
  - Sustainable financial backing?
  - Economy: home, abroad?
  - Seasonality, weather effects?

Let's go back to Trevor's Terrific Travel Ltd. They identified their key internal strengths and weaknesses and looked at the main opportunities and threats that exist in the external environment that they operate in:

- *Strengths:*
  - Two prime-site locations in a major British city.
  - Lots of staff have face-to-face customer contact.
  - A computer network has been installed connecting the two offices.
  - The ICT systems are well developed.
  - Increased financial pressures mean a merger shares infrastructure costs.
  - Both parties have different expertise and it is important to focus on this rather than for each to try to do everything.
  - Resources will be organized more effectively.
- *Weaknesses:*
  - Closer collaboration may prove to be a slow process thanks to the practical difficulties of pooling resources and reluctance by some managers to give up their independence.
  - Decisions can take twice as long as usual because one of the problems can be who will take overall responsibility for a

project. There is always a danger in joint working that, unless someone is put in overall charge, responsibilities fall between two stools.

– It is not easy because different organizations will have different ways of working.

– It is important to be clear from the outset what the goals of the collaboration are and that there must be agreed protocols governing practical issues such as how often meetings will be held between the two organizations, what they will cover and who will chair them.

- *Opportunities:*
  – Regional Development Agency funding available for SMEs for development of their e-business.
  – A merger would mean more buying power, therefore cheaper holidays and so more business.
  – A merger would mean joint administration; therefore either staff numbers could be cut or staff could be freed up to take on other duties to expand the business.
  – Today's internet includes not only browsing from a desktop or laptop computer, but also surfing with web TV, palm pilots, mobile phones and other net-connected devices. We need to make our pages accessible bearing in mind that not all of the visitors to the site will be viewing it on a monitor and navigating with a mouse. A clear, well-formatted site, with easy words, can make it easier on everyone.

- *Threats:*
  – We must be sure that the two companies are completely compatible. Not only should these organizations and customer bases complement each other, but we must also be certain that the two workforces can work together successfully.
  – There may be ramifications (legal, tax, employment, etc) attached to merging that would make a merger counter-productive.
  – We need to consider the impact on our customer base. We should not assume that all our customers will automatically stay with the merged company.
  – At all times, we need to keep our staff informed. There will be rumours anyway because staff will be concerned about their positions and their job security. We must consult with them and inform them of decisions as they are made.

Again, going back to the areas you should cover, and using the example above, write down SWOT issues for your own business. Identify your key strengths and weaknesses and, going back to your PEST analysis, look at the main opportunities and threats that exist in the external environment that you operate in:

● *Strengths:*

_____

_____

_____

_____

● *Weaknesses:*

_____

_____

_____

_____

● *Threats:*

_____

_____

_____

_____

If you're having problems thinking of things, below are some examples that you can 'borrow' and apply to your own situation:

● *Strengths:*
    – End-user sales control and direction.
    – Right products, quality and reliability.
    – Superior product performance versus competitors.
    – Better product life and durability.
    – Spare manufacturing capacity.
    – Some staff have experience of end-user sector.
    – Have customer lists.

- – Direct delivery capability.
- – Product innovations ongoing.
- – Can serve from existing sites.
- – Products have required accreditations.
- – Processes and IT should cope.
- – Management is committed and confident.
- *Weaknesses:*
  - – Customer lists not tested.
  - – Some gaps in range for certain sectors.
  - – We would be a small player.
  - – No direct marketing experience.
  - – We cannot supply end-users abroad.
  - – Need more sales people.
  - – Limited budget.
  - – No pilot or trial done yet.
  - – Don't have a detailed plan yet.
  - – Delivery staff need training.
  - – Customer service staff need training.
  - – Processes and systems, etc.
  - – Management cover insufficient.
- *Threats:*
  - – Legislation could impact.
  - – Environmental effects would favour larger competitors.
  - – Existing core business distribution risk.
  - – Market demand very seasonal.
  - – Retention of key staff critical.
  - – Could distract from core business.
  - – Possible negative publicity.
  - – Vulnerable to reactive attack by major competitors.

But wait! What about the opportunities? No, we haven't forgotten about it. Go back to your PEST analysis and look at the two main headings that you picked out in each category. Take each point and associate three opportunities with it, thereby identifying opportunities that you can take advantage of in your current environment:

- *Political:*
  Point 1:

  _____

  _____

  _____

  Point 2:

  _____

  _____

  _____

- *Economic:*
  Point 1:

  _____

  _____

  _____

  Point 2:

  _____

  _____

  _____

- *Sociocultural:*
  Point 1:

  _____

  _____

  _____

  Point 2:

  _____

  _____

  _____

- *Technological:*
  Point 1:

  _____

  _____

  _____

  Point 2:

  _____

  _____

  _____

Again, if you're struggling for inspiration, use the following suggestions and apply them to your situation:

- *Opportunities:*
  - Could develop new products.
  - Local competitors have poor products.
  - Profit margins will be good.
  - End-users respond to new ideas.
  - Could extend to overseas.
  - New specialist applications.
  - Can surprise competitors.
  - Support core business.

Your strengths and weaknesses

You should now have a list of the strengths and weaknesses of your business, and a useful set of opportunities that you have identified to take advantage of changes in the outside world that affect your business. We are on the home straight and are well on the way to giving you an important set of objectives to work to. What we need to do now is to take your strengths and weaknesses and to determine which ones are fundamental and which ones are just marginal. Table 3.1 shows the fundamental and marginal strengths and weaknesses for Trevor's Terrific Travel Ltd.

You should now take *your* strengths and weaknesses and decide which ones fit into which box in Table 3.2.

Table 3.1 Strengths and weaknesses of Trevor's Terrific Travel Ltd

Fundamental strength	Fundamental weakness	Marginal strength	Marginal weakness	Neutral
Two prime-site locations in a major British city.	Closer collaboration may prove to be a slow process thanks to the practical difficulties of pooling resources and reluctance by some managers to give up their independence.	Lots of staff have face-to-face customer contact.	Decisions can take twice as long as usual because one of the problems can be who will take overall responsibility for a project.	Resources will be organized more effectively.
A computer network has been installed connecting the two offices.	It is not easy because different organizations will have different ways of working.	Increased financial pressures mean a merger shares infrastructure costs.		It is important to be clear from the outset what the goals of the collaboration are.
The ICT systems are well developed.		Both parties have different expertise and it is important to focus on this rather than for each to try to do everything.		

This is where we take your *fundamental* strengths and match them up with the *opportunities* that you have identified. Why? Simple: you should always play to your strengths! You are bound to have found some opportunities in the outside world that are perfect for you to use your best strengths in. If you use your strengths in well-thought-out opportunities, then you are bound to succeed!

Table 3.2 Your strengths and weaknesses

Fundamental strength	Fundamental weakness	Marginal strength	Marginal weakness	Neutral

Table 3.3 on page 98 shows how Trevor's Terrific Travel Ltd did it. Now it's your turn. In Table 3.4, relate your business's fundamental strengths to outside opportunities that you have identified in your PEST analysis.

Table 3.3 Matching strengths and opportunities for Trevor's Terrific Travel Ltd

Strengths	Opportunities
Two prime-site locations in a major British city.	There is a bias towards higher socio-economic groups (ABs), and the types of holidays that the company sells are popular with both young adults and active retired people (these economic groups being found mainly in the more prosperous cities).
A computer network has been installed connecting the two offices.	The developments in information communication technologies (ICTs) and the internet in particular have revolutionized the entire tourism industry.
The ICT systems are well developed.	Business tourism fluctuates with the strength of the economy (business customers want ease of booking above all else). Also, there is a current skills shortage in the industry and e-learning could be a key issue.

Table 3.4 Matching your strengths and opportunities

Strengths	Opportunities

Your objectives

Now it's time to show that it has all been worth it – the objectives! So why are objectives so important? Hasn't this been a lot of trouble just to get some objectives? Let's go back to 1953 when a questionnaire was circulated to the graduating seniors at Yale University. They were asked the question, 'Do you have clear, specific, written objectives for your life, and have you developed complete plans for their accomplishment after you leave this university?'

The results of the survey were surprising. Only 3 per cent of the seniors had clear, written goals and plans for what they wanted to do when they left university. A further 13 per cent had objectives, but had not written them down. The other 84 per cent had no objectives at all, except to get out of university and enjoy the summer.

Twenty years later, in 1973, the surviving members of that Yale graduating class were surveyed again. Among other questions, they were asked, 'What is your net worth today?'

When they totalled and averaged the results of this survey, they found that the 3 per cent who had clear, written objectives and plans when they left the university 20 years before were worth more, in dollar terms, than the other 97 per cent put together! And *objective setting* was the only characteristic that the top 3 per cent had in common. Some had earned good grades and some had received poor grades. Some had worked in one industry and some in another. Some had moved across the country and some had stayed in the same city. The one common denominator of the most successful graduates was that they had put together their achievable objectives right from the very beginning.

Some people believe that objectives are unnecessary and that it is best to let business life unfold in a random manner. But if your business could be compared to a fast and reliable car, then setting objectives is about putting you in the driving seat and deciding where you are going. It is important, though, not to get so hung up on the destination that you don't enjoy the journey along the way.

An objective is like a dream with a date on it. Having a clear direction of where you are going is a statement that you are taking responsibility for your business. You will then welcome the forces of universal intelligence to rally to your cause. There is a nice quote from the poet and playwright Goethe on this point: 'The moment one definitely commits oneself, then providence moves too. All sorts of things occur to help one that would not otherwise occur... whatever you can do or dream you can, begin it. Boldness has genius, power and magic in it, begin it now.'

It is important at all times to know what you want. This is like the fuel that keeps you moving forward. Without stating what you want, you will stall, stagnate and get stuck in a rut. It is sometimes very difficult for people to know what they want. This is where the following exercise comes in, which, although you probably don't realize yet, is vital to your business. But before we get stuck in, just consider these three famous quotes:

- 'If one does not know to which port one is sailing, no wind is favourable' (Seneca).
- 'All successful people have a goal. No one can get anywhere unless he knows where he wants to go and what he wants to be or do' (Norman Vincent Peale, *The Power of Positive Thinking*).
- 'Emptiness is a symptom of not living creatively. You either have not a goal that is important or you are not using your talents and efforts in striving towards an important goal' (Maxwell Maltz).

We now have the basis for a campaign aimed at improving your business's reputation and stakeholder management by playing on identified opportunities that have been matched with your company's main strengths. A simple acronym used to set objectives is SMART. The purpose of objectives is to provide a definition of success and to provide it up front, so that everyone understands what needs to be done. Good objectives have five important properties. To remember them, good objectives need to be SMART:

- *Specific:* Objectives need to describe particular actions and results in quantifiable terms. For example, let's imagine a widget factory manager who is given the very vague objective from higher up to 'increase production'. To make this objective more specific, she might change it to 'increase widget output by 3 per cent'.
- *Measurable:* This means that each objective must have some sort of mechanism in place to check the extent to which it is getting achieved. If our factory manager doesn't already have something in place to count the number of widgets produced, then she'd better find something to do so.
- *Achievable:* The objective needs to be possible to accomplish with a reasonable time and energy investment from all team members. This may seem obvious, but there are plenty of times that impossible objectives get set, often because the manager who set them didn't know enough to realize they were impossible and didn't consult with anyone who did. Our factory manager may wish to meet with workers and their supervisors to discover whether the 3 per cent output increase is reasonable or not before she imposes it.

- *Relevant:* The objective must be meaningful to all team members and it must be something they are able to influence. Presumably the factory workers under our manager are able to influence the widget output: setting individual objectives, like five more widgets a day per person, makes the whole thing relevant. Had our manager asked them to 'increase profit margins' then she would have been greeted by blank stares. Relevance is, of course, determined by the people the objective is being set *for*.
- *Time-bound:* The objective needs a deadline or no one's ever going to get around to accomplishing it. Our factory manager should change her objective to 'increase widget production by 3 per cent *in two months*' to make it conform to this properly.

SMART objectives can be used in all areas of a business, for example:

- *Profitability objectives:* to achieve a 20 per cent return on capital employed by August 2007.
- *Market share objectives:* to gain 25 per cent of the market for sports shoes by September 2008.
- *Promotional objectives:* to increase awareness of the dangers of AIDS in France from 12 per cent to 25 per cent by June 2007.
- *Objectives for survival:* to survive the current double-dip recession.
- *Objectives for growth:* to increase the size of our German operation from £200,000 in 2005 to £400,000 in 2006.
- *Objectives for branding:* to make Y brand of bottled beer the preferred brand of 21- to 28-year-old females in North America by February 2006.

There are many examples of objectives. Be careful not to confuse objectives with goals and aims. Goals and aims tend to be more vague and focus on the longer term. They will not be SMART. However, many objectives start off as aims or goals and therefore they are of equal importance.

If we now look at the objectives of Trevor's Terrific Travel Ltd, we'll see how their SMART objectives are reached by framing SMART objectives to the strengths and opportunities that they have just married up:

1. To market our high street stores so that 10,000 AB customers buy holidays from us by September 2006.
2. To continue to develop our IT infrastructure so that all our suppliers are communicated with by intranet by December 2006.
3. To develop our website so that 5,000 business customers use us by September 2006.
4. To develop our ICT systems so that we have a full in-house computerized training programme that trains 30 new recruits by July 2006.

These objectives are specific, measurable, achievable and relevant and have deadlines. They also have an enormous element of PR attached to them. You now have to do the same thing: take your strengths and opportunities table, which you have filled in, and turn them into meaningful objectives:

1.

_____

_____

_____

2.

_____

_____

_____

3.

_____

_____

_____

If you're struggling to put the different elements of your SMART objectives together, then the following may help:

- *Specific:* Is there a description of a precise or specific behaviour or outcome that is linked to a rate, number, percentage or frequency?
- *Measurable:* Is there a reliable system in place to measure progress towards the achievement of the objective?

- *Achievable:* With a reasonable amount of effort and application can the objective be achieved?
- *Relevant:* Can the people with whom the objective is set make an impact on the situation? Do they have the necessary knowledge, authority and skill?
- *Time-bound:* Is there a finish and/or a start date clearly stated or defined?

Conclusion

All that effort for three objectives! But the important thing is that they are the right objectives for your business and will play a big role in your future success. And things are really starting to come together now: you know where you are; you know what key people think about you; you have a strategic direction and now a set of objectives. We have the bones of your future success; now all we need to do is put the meat on them...

4 Looking after your stakeholders

Introduction

This is where we look at how the business is going to identify the people who are going to help it realize these goals. It looks at their expectations and shows how to identify which ones carry the most power and interest in what your business is trying to achieve. The use of the internet will also be shown as a key tool in the PR battle, and suggestions for its design will be given.

Stakeholders

You now have a good set of objectives. All you need is the small matter of carrying them out. The way to do this is to produce a set of *tactics* that will ensure the success of your *strategy*. In PR the way you do this is to focus on your *stakeholders*: these are the people who are going to help you to realize your objectives.

For those of you who skipped Chapter 2, the following is an important point. Your business operates in an increasingly complex and ever-changing environment, and outside pressures, not just commercial ones, affect your organization on many differing levels, and all are interrelated (see Figure 4.1).

You cannot control this environment, nor can you control the hearts and minds of your many stakeholders. What you can and should do,

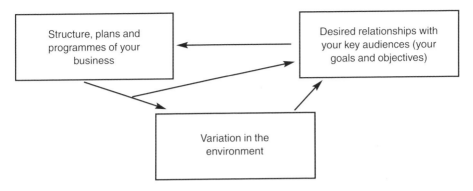

Figure 4.1 Pressures affecting the organization

however, is to create a mutual understanding between yourself as an organization and the key players that you need to influence. You need to communicate with these groups through genuine two-way processes, so that not only are these people aware of what you are trying to achieve, but also you learn about genuine concerns *and are ready to adjust your behaviour and decisions according to these concerns.*

This is a key point: it should not be looked at as taking away your right to manage your own business, but it should be looked at as responding and evolving according to the needs and desires of these major audiences who influence your organization and ultimately decide whether it thrives and survives.

When things aren't going well, public relations must become crisis management. But if a business goes into a crisis with a good reputation and solid relationships with its constituents and the media, the job is infinitely easier. A strong reputation is like an insurance policy: money in the bank for a rainy day. It probably won't help a firm avoid a nasty story in the newspaper, but it may keep it to a one-day story rather than the continued haemorrhaging in the media that can take a toll on a company's sales. Business experience and research have shown time and again that a good reputation helps a company sell its products, recruit the best and the brightest, and attract the most valuable business partners.

A stakeholder is any person, group or institution that has an interest in what your business does. This definition includes both those whom you intend to be affected by what you do, such as your suppliers or customers, *and* those you do not intend to influence but who *are* affected in some way, such as local residents near your business premises or the local authority.

Stakeholders can be divided into two very broad groups: 1) primary stakeholders – those who are directly affected by what you do, ie who expect to benefit from (eg customers) or be adversely affected by (eg competitors) what you do; 2) secondary stakeholders – those with some intermediary role. These might include trade unions, banks, local government, export promotion agencies and business service providers.

On the face of it, this might not sound particularly relevant: who cares who is primary or secondary? But there is, in fact, an important distinction to be made. This is because your *key stakeholders* – those who are the most important to you when trying to realize your objectives – can be from either group. In other words, people who are 'secondary stakeholders', those who would not really have much of a direct relationship with you, could actually prove very important to you.

Different sets of people are affected by any one issue. From this perspective, there is no such thing as the 'general public'. Everyone is different and everything the business does affects different people in different ways. And similarly, what these people say and do affects what happens to your business.

Stakeholder analysis

'Stakeholder analysis' (SA) sounds like one of those pie-in-the-sky academic terms that mean very little in the real world. In fact, the origins of SA belong to the history of business and management. This is reflected in the term 'stakeholder' itself, apparently first recorded in 1708 to mean a deposit. The word now refers to *anyone significantly affecting or affected by someone else's decision-making activity*.

The notion of stakeholder relations goes back to the beginnings of industrialism and is embedded in ideals of the 19th-century cooperative movement. It reappears in business and management discussions throughout the 1930s. The approach was then designed, and continues to be used nowadays, by firms to factor in stakeholder interests in order to enhance the business's relationship with society and secure better prospects of financial success. With the help of SA, firm decisions can profit from views that go beyond the narrow interests of stockholders and shareholders investing in a business.

But there is more to SA than new wine emerging from old bottles. It also has the advantage of being flexible, and helps focus attention on specific problems and opportunities for change. SA is about the identification of a business's key players, an assessment of their interests, and the ways in which those interests affect business viability. It identifies the goals and roles of different groups, and helps to formulate the best ways of engaging with these groups.

SA establishes which groups to work with, and sets out an approach so this can be achieved. In particular a stakeholder analysis can be used to:

- identify and define the characteristics of key stakeholders;
- draw out the interests of stakeholders in relation to the problems that your business is seeking to address;
- identify conflicts of interests between stakeholders, and to help manage such relationships during the course of your business objectives;
- help to identify relations between stakeholders that may enable 'coalitions';
- assess the capacity of different stakeholders and stakeholder groups to participate;
- help to assess the appropriate type of participation by different stakeholders at successive stages of the business cycle, eg informing, consulting, partnership.

When conducting a stakeholder analysis, we need to get the crux of the following questions:

- Who are your key stakeholders?
- What are the goals, motivations and interests of your key stakeholders?
- What is the power and influence of each key stakeholder?
- What is the importance or impact of each key stakeholder to your business objectives?
- What are the participation roles of each key stakeholder to your business objectives?
- How can you work with each stakeholder for win–win outcomes?

Firstly, then, you need to list who your stakeholders are. There are eight basic key stakeholder groups that need to be serviced:

1. the community at large or people living near or affected by your business's plant, premises or practices;

2. employees, managers and their unions;
3. customers – past, present and future;
4. suppliers of materials and non-financial services;
5. the money market, including shareholders, banks, insurers and investors;
6. distributors, agents, wholesalers and retailers;
7. potential employees, consultants and agents;
8. opinion leaders, particularly radio, television, press and other media professionals or activists, including lobbyists and environmental pressure groups.

These will be important groups as not only will many of them recognize the important issues surrounding your new business objectives, but many will organize themselves to face these issues. The job of your PR campaign should be to ensure they approach all of your issues positively predisposed to your business and willing to see things from your point of view.

Example

Big Car Manufacturers plc were planning to close down car production in one of their plants in Anytown. Instead they would use the facility to research a new breed of diesel engines, but this would employ only a fraction of the current workforce. A sticky PR problem indeed – shedding so many jobs would not be good for their image. So the first thing they did was to list their stakeholders:

- *Consumer stakeholders:*
  - customers: past, present and future;
  - Association of British Insurers;
  - Automobile Association (AA);
  - British International Motor Show organizers;
  - Cherished Numbers Dealers Association;
  - Confederation of British Industry;
  - Consumers Association;
  - Federation Internationale de l'Automobile (FIA);
  - Institute of Advanced Motorists;
  - Motor Industry Research Association;
  - Royal Automobile Club (RAC);
  - Society of Motor Manufacturers and Traders Ltd (SMMT).

- *Government stakeholders:*
    - Department for Work and Pensions (DWP);
    - Department of Transport;
    - Department of Trade and Industry (DTI);
    - Driver and Vehicle Licensing Agency;
    - Health and Safety Executive;
    - Office for National Statistics;
    - Office of Fair Trading (OFT);
    - Vehicle Inspectorate.
- *Other stakeholders:*
    - the community at large or people living near or affected by the Anytown's plant's premises or practices;
    - employees, managers and their unions: TUC, TGWU, MSF;
    - suppliers of materials and non-financial services;
    - the money market, including shareholders, banks, insurers and investors: London Stock Exchange, Barclays Bank, Lloyds TSB, Bank of Scotland, Royal Bank of Scotland and HSBC;
    - distributors, agents, wholesalers and retailers;
    - potential employees, consultants and agents;
    - opinion leaders, particularly radio, television, press and other media professionals or activists;
    - lobbyists and environmental pressure groups: Friends of the Earth; Greenpeace; local environmental groups.
- *Other vehicle manufacturer stakeholders:*
    - Alfa Romeo (GB) Ltd;
    - Aston Martin;
    - Audi;
    - BMW (GB) Ltd;
    - Citroën;
    - Daewoo;
    - Honda;
    - Jaguar;
    - etc...

Now it's your turn! List stakeholders in your business under the following headings:

- *Consumer stakeholders:*

_____

_____

_____

_____

- *Government stakeholders:*

_____

_____

_____

_____

- *Other stakeholders:*

_____

_____

_____

_____

- *Competitor stakeholders:*

_____

_____

_____

_____

Taking into account these stakeholders, Big Car Manufacturers plc narrowed their list down to 12 *key* stakeholders for the following reasons:

1. *Employees:* They have a stake in the success of the company and are key to this.
2. *Politicians:* As the plant is such an important employer, political support for the decision is vital. The cutbacks at the plant have serious political repercussions, and it became obvious that political

support would be key to any of Big Car Manufacturers plc future decisions. Trade and Industry and Employment ministers will need to be targeted, as well as the mayor and local MP.

3. *Other car manufacturers:* The clarity of new car prices could continue to generate negative publicity for the UK new car market as a whole, and it is in the interests of all manufacturers to address this issue.
4. *Consumers:* As well as new car pricing issues, the costs of running a car are making car travel less desirable, which has a direct impact on the sales of all cars in the UK. Garnering this support could prove invaluable.
5. *Environmental groups:* In terms of both the car manufacturing process and emissions issues, local and national pressure groups need to be engaged.
6. *Technical and trade press:* New technologies will be important to the sale of new cars. To communicate these innovations we need to engage those who will adopt and champion these technologies at an early stage.
7. *Community leaders:* Support from the local community will be key in ensuring that grass-roots opinion can influence any political decisions that may be made and would affect the plant's future.
8. *Banks:* Financial support will be vital if the plant is to have a long-term future as this will require more investment.
9. *Shareholders:* These are, at the end of the day, the group that own the company.
10. *Mainstream media:* Genuine understanding of issues facing the plant would enable the plant to take decisions without sensationalist and ill-informed media fallout.
11. *Suppliers:* In essence, this group needs to know that the plant will be able to pay its bills, which means it can keep manufacturing goods.
12. *Dealers:* These need to know that there will be a product for them to sell and exactly what products they will be able to sell.

Now list *your* key stakeholders, in order of importance, and say why they are important to you:

1. _____
2. _____

3. _____

4. _____

5. _____

6. _____

7. _____

8. _____

9. _____

10. _____

11. _____

12. _____

It is vital that you recognize that stakeholders and your business have consequences for each other: stakeholders create consequences for the very environment that you trade in, which includes your products and services, your company policies, your business practices, your ideas and your objectives. In turn, you have an impact on the lives of your workers and the workers of other companies that supply you, the businesses that sell your products, your customers, etc.

Stakeholders' expectations

Then you need to address the following questions: What do the key stakeholders you have identified expect of your business? What are their pains, concerns and desires that can be regarded as leverage points that can be used to hear the messages that you need to communicate in order to meet your objectives?

Big Car Manufacturers plc asked the same questions and came up with the following:

1. *Employees:* They would have an extremely high level of interest in any future campaign as, frankly, their livelihoods depend on the success of the plant. They have a high level of ability to influence the campaign as, without their support and continued effort in maintaining or increasing production, the plant will cease to be. Potential employees will also be key, as skilled workers will be needed to operate the new diesel engine facility.

2. *Politicians:* These would want to see a prosperous plant as this means jobs and prosperity for their constituency and the UK economy as a whole. As such, they would have a high interest in the campaign and could affect its outcomes by showing support in the media or changing legislation to help the plant.

3. *Other car manufacturers:* These want to see a thriving car market, but would only have an interest in any campaign from the point of view of competitors. They would see the issue of car-pricing policy as something to be addressed through a car manufacturer representative body.

4. *Consumers:* Customers would expect to see lower car prices and a better standard of cars. They would have minimal interest in the campaign, as they would see it as yet more corporate 'selling', but they have a huge ability to influence the outcomes of the strategy as, being the customers, they have enormous power regarding the way the plant's reputation is perceived.

5. *Environmental groups:* These groups want to see companies being environmentally responsible. They form an important part of public opinion through acting as a watchdog for ethical consumers. As such, they would have a high level of interest in the environmental aspects of alternatives fuels in the campaign, although a weak ability to influence its outcomes.

6. *Technical and trade press:* This category expects to hear news of automobile innovations, which makes good copy for them. They would only be interested in any campaign from the point of view of product information they could gain from it, although their importance in pushing this out to people who could adopt it and champion it at an early stage is vitally important.

7. *Community leaders:* They want to see a successful plant that will continue to provide employment and service opportunities for local businesses. They would have an interest in the campaign from this perspective, and their grass-roots opinion could help when influencing political decisions.

8. *Banks:* They simply expect a return on their investment, and would have minimal interest in any strategy, as long as their financial returns were realized. However, their financial support would be vital in securing potential investment for the exploitation of new technologies developed by the plant.

9. *Shareholders:* Like banks, they expect a return on investment. Again, they would not have a particular interest in a specific

campaign, but they would need to give their backing to management should the plant decide to focus on a particular area of business, eg advanced fuel development.

10. *Mainstream media:* They expect good stories, but operate in a very short-term news environment. They would not be interested in any campaign that was not immediately and inherently newsworthy. However, it is vital that they are properly informed about any future decisions made at the plant to avoid bad publicity and adverse news stories that may be ill informed and sensationalist.

11. *Suppliers:* They expect the company to keep placing orders with them and to get paid for the goods and services they provide. They would not have a particular interest in the campaign, and would not have a great deal of influence over its outcomes.

12. *Dealers:* They expect to have a good product to be able to sell to customers. They would have an acute interest in new product development that they could market, although they would not have that much influence over the campaign other than trying to push a new development to customers to encourage them to try it out and become its 'champions'.

Using this example, think about what your stakeholders will expect of your business when you start to implement your new objectives:

1. _____

2. _____

3. _____

4. _____

5. _____

6. _____

7. _____

8. _____

9. _____

10. _____

11. _____

12. _____

Stakeholder mapping

After looking at stakeholders in relation to the extent to which they are likely to show interest in any strategy, we can look at the type of relationship that we need to establish with each stakeholder group. The following is a useful tool that does two major things: 1) gauges how much power your stakeholders actually hold over what you want to achieve; 2) looks at how interested they will be in what you are trying to achieve.

You firstly need to look at the situation you have at present. Big Car Manufacturers plc looked at their stakeholders and judged that they lay in the boxes shown in Figure 4.2.

Here we can see that Big Car Manufacturers plc think that other car manufacturers don't have much interest in what is going on in their Anytown plant, but they don't have much power in this respect either. Their consumers, however, have a lot of power, but don't have that much interest ('Car plants are closing down all the time'). Likewise, banks and the media have a high level of power, but not much interest despite the odd story here and there. Those with high levels of power and interest are politicians and the affected employees.

Taking this tool, use Figure 4.3 to see if you can judge where your stakeholders should be.

	Low	Level of interest	High
Low (Level of power)	Other car manufacturers Suppliers		Environmental groups Community leaders Dealers
High	Consumers Technical and trade press Banks Shareholders Mainstream media		Employees Politicians

Figure 4.2 Interest and power of Big Car Manufacturers plc stakeholders

Low
Level of interest
High
Low
Level of power
High

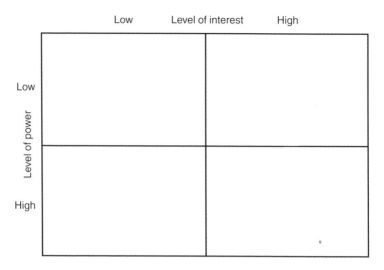

Figure 4.3 Interest and power of your stakeholders

Big Car Manufacturers plc then map out what they *want* the situation with their key stakeholders to look like (Figure 4.4).

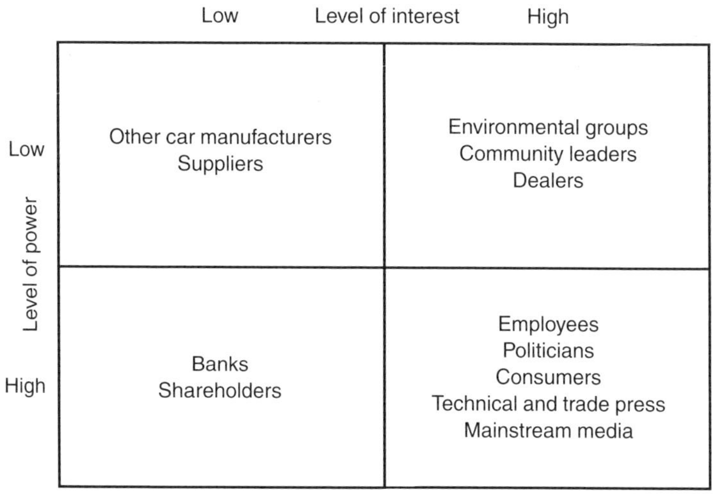

Low
Level of interest
High
Low
Level of power
High
Other car manufacturers
Suppliers
Environmental groups
Community leaders
Dealers
Banks
Shareholders
Employees
Politicians
Consumers
Technical and trade press
Mainstream media

Figure 4.4 Desired interest and power of Big Car Manufacturers plc stakeholders

Now you should do the same thing. If you are to have a successful relationship with all major stakeholders, the situation should look like the one you create using Figure 4.5.

Low
Level of interest
High
Low
Level of power
High

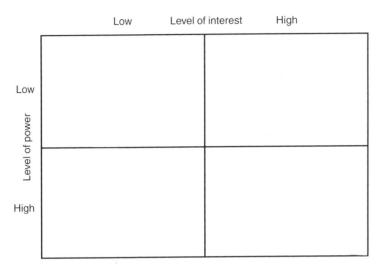

Figure 4.5 Desired interest and power of your stakeholders

Before we move on, there's one small adjustment to make. Transfer the information from Table 4.5 and put it in the same boxes in Table 4.6.

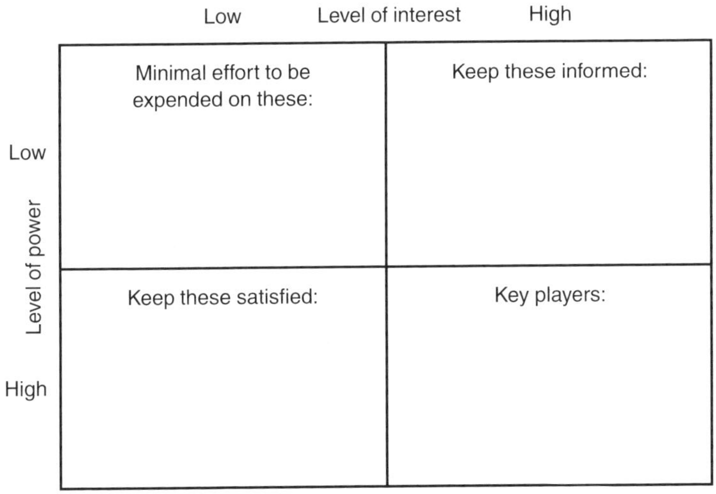

Low
Level of interest
High
Minimal effort to be expended on these:
Keep these informed:
Low
Level of power
High
Keep these satisfied:
Key players:

Figure 4.6 A stakeholder strategy

Voilà! A stakeholder strategy to rival anything your more illustrious competitors could come up with. It is important that we raise the level of interest of powerful stakeholders through good information and briefing. Similarly, the needs of stakeholders that we should keep satisfied also have to be properly addressed, largely through information. They can be crucially important 'allies' in influencing the attitudes of more powerful stakeholders through PR.

What your stakeholders think

From the above it is clear that we need to develop a campaign to reposition certain stakeholders and to identify who are the key blockers of change and how we can respond to them in terms of education. We also have to maintain levels of interest among key players in order to ensure successful implementation of the campaign.

To do this repositioning, we need to compare the current and desired positions of stakeholders as outlined above, identify the mismatches and establish what our priority groups need to be. Big Car Manufacturers plc performed this task and came up with the picture shown in Table 4.1.

By performing the same task, list in Table 4.2 what you think your key stakeholders think and what you would like them to think.

Messages

We have discussed where we are starting from in terms of reputation, and we have established the stakeholder audiences we need to reach. Now we must consider the messages that we need to send them, how we want them to respond and when we need them to react.

What are the messages by audience?

Before looking at what messages need to be sent to which stakeholders, we need to consider a range of issues, such as the manipulative factors that we can use to promote this two-way stakeholder–organization relationship, through the messages that we send, the medium through which we send them and who we use to communicate them.

Table 4.1 Establishing priority groups at Big Car Manufacturers plc

Priority	Stakeholder	Thinks now	Should think
1.	Employees	'Is my future secure at this plant?'	'This plant has a bright future.'
2.	Consumers	'This plant is in trouble, and why should I buy from a company that treats its workers so badly?'	'This plant produces innovative products and has a skilled, dedicated workforce.'
3.	Mainstream media	'The fall of a once great company makes a great story.'	'The plant is an important one to the economy and should be supported.'
4.	Technical and trade press	'The plant just churns out pretty standard car equipment in a very crowded market.'	'The plant produces very innovative products that we need to cover.'
5.	Politicians	'Although they are an important employer, they should start treating their workers better.'	'They are a major employer and treat staff well, and they need whatever support government can give.'
6.	Shareholders	'They appear to be in long-term difficulty so I might consider selling my shares.'	'They have identified gaps in a competitive market, so they are a good investment.'
7.	Banks	'They appear to be a company in trouble so we shouldn't consider lending them any more money.'	'They have a good long-term commercial plan with solid support, so we should lend them money.'
8.	Environmental groups	'Car manufacturers destroy the environment with both their products and the making of their products.'	'This plant uses processing methods that should be held up as an example to the industry, along with the environmentally friendly cars they produce.'
9.	Dealers	'I don't know if we will even be selling their cars in the future.'	'There are a lot of new products coming out and we have to think about the best way to sell them.'
10.	Community leaders	'The plant has let us down with all its lay-offs and will take a lot of money out of the local economy.'	'The plant has a bright future, and the new diesel centre could turn into a large complex bringing in even more skilled jobs.'
11.	Suppliers	'How long before the plant stops ordering from us?'	'We can improve our own processes now we know that the plant has a bright future and orders will continue to be made.'
12.	Other car manufacturers	'Big Car Manufacturers plc is in trouble and we should capitalize on this and kill it off as a competitor.'	'Big Car Manufacturers plc will be an important player for a long time to come, and we need to work with them to ensure the health of the car market in the UK.'

Table 4.2 Establishing your priority groups

Priority	Stakeholder	Thinks now	Should think
1.			
2.			
3.			
4.			
5.			
6.			
7.			
8.			
9.			
10.			
11.			
12.			

We need to look at how we will select which channel through which to communicate to them. We need to look at costs, how feasible it is to manage the channel and whether it is sustainable over time.

We then need to look at how we want these stakeholders to change: with some stakeholders we just want to increase recognition of the issues facing your business. In others we want to create values in favour of the actions of your business. This is important as at present we do not want actually to change the actions and behaviour of people, which would have implications in terms of strategy and cost.

The people we use to communicate our messages are also of vital importance. Because we know our stakeholders, we can specialize in concentrating on parts of the audience as we know their needs and interests. Because of our two-way interaction, you must not fall into the trap of deciding to tell them only what *you* think they should know: you need to let them ask the questions and not simply offer them messages that you think will please them.

How do we want the audiences to respond?

The overall benefit of the approach of engaging stakeholders is that, for the first time, you will be able to set the 'public opinion' agenda. Because of the breadth of knowledge that you will be imparting to key audiences across society, you will be able to create a properly informed media, public and policy agenda. People will no longer be lumped with a 'sensational' story about your business and react accordingly: they will already know exactly why your organization is pursuing the path it is, and will pass on this knowledge to others.

This is ultimately the way you want your audiences to respond: in effect, to become channels themselves through which to pass on your objectives' messages. The problem for any organization is that it is not feasible to engage with the entire population all of the time, to do so 'just in case' some may be influenced by an issue related to the plant.

What you are doing is the targeting of key stakeholders in a genuine two-way relationship not only to become positively predisposed to your business's values and thus less likely to form negative views, but also to pass on information to colleagues. For example, if we take Big Car Manufacturers plc, any political debate regarding the plant would see a stakeholder MP having a good background knowledge of issues relating to the plant, about which the MP would inform other MPs, political researchers, the media, etc.

In other cases, key stakeholders will choose relevant parts of messages, reframe them in language understandable to others and communicate them to other stakeholders who are less of a priority. And while some issues may not affect some key stakeholders, such as your business implementing Investors in People, this information could be of interest to others, so key stakeholders would still communicate this even though they were not the specific target audience for the message.

Starting from the point of view that audiences will usually seek out the messages that they want – the messages that have the most gratifying content for them – we need to develop an active information campaign. Merely publishing information, for example on a website for people to access, is not good enough. We need to actively help stakeholders locate the information that they want. This will be a key part of your stakeholder strategy and will enable them to pass on information.

When do we need them to react?

The basis of a good stakeholder campaign is one built around developing relationships and trust. Educating people about values may take a long time, but although there is a long build-up there are also long-term effects.

Getting your messages across

In Chapter 5 we will be looking in detail at the various and imaginative forms in which your messages can be got across. In this chapter, however, we will specifically be focusing on the internet and its uses, as this is a particular piece of infrastructure that you will need to get in place before you launch your PR campaign. Whichever strategic direction you choose, the internet will undoubtedly play a big part in it.

Unfortunately, many of the best PR plans fall apart because a website just isn't up to the job. Here we look at the most important considerations, and only when you are happy with your site compared to what is outlined here should you embark on your PR campaign.

E-PR

There's an old saying that goes: 'When all you have is a hammer, everything looks like a nail.' Sometimes it is said in a derogatory way, implying that the person is not looking for the 'correct' tool. But what is fascinating about the internet is that it is so general-purpose that we can successfully find ways to use it for a wide variety of things, often ones not foreseen even by its creators. Tools that can be used for many different and important things often become very popular.

The car caught on so well because of its general-purpose nature. First used for recreation, taking you out to the 'country', it could also be used in rural areas to go into town or visit friends, for commuting in suburban and urban areas, visiting people at great distances, as part of work, as a means for status or 'freedom', etc. No other means of transportation met as many needs during the years when we built up much of society around it.

And so it appears to be with the internet. The first and most obvious accepted use is as a communications tool with people you already know. E-mail and instant messaging have gone way past the early adopter phase. For many businesses, e-mail has become one of the dominant forms of communication. It is up there with the telephone and visiting, and more and more is displacing physical mail and fax. This is pretty amazing. It took the telephone years to reach this level of acceptance for such mundane uses. Fax *never* reached it for personal uses.

How to set up a virtual press office

If you have a website, or are thinking of setting one up, then a virtual press office (VPO) will be of great importance in helping communicate information about your company and its products and services.

Your VPO should contain all the information about your company that you don't want a journalist to get from somewhere else. Depending on the nature of your business, this might include: company history, management profiles, research and statistics, financial reports or product information.

A traditional press office provides journalists with key data that help them write their stories. PR professionals working in these offices distribute background information, news releases, press packs, images and other useful materials. They also communicate directly with the media and arrange events such as interviews with key contacts.

A VPO is both a cost- and time-effective method of extending the capabilities of a traditional press office via the internet. By utilizing today's technology and taking into account the evolving requirements of journalists, a VPO should help you provide a more effective service to the media.

However, be aware that many virtual press centres miss the mark by wasting time with rambling news releases and stories that are centred on pure promotion. Overbearing corporate-speak in online press material generates cynical reporting, which in turn ensures there will be no repeat visits to a company's site.

A good VPO provides a 24-hour service and instant access to information while usefully automating many of the time-consuming aspects of PR. Today almost all journalists use the internet for some aspect of their research. The majority specifically use company websites as a source of information, and this represents an excellent opportunity to get your message directly to the media via your website.

There are a number of important rules to remember when setting up a VPO. People get lost easily, so include a 'return home' link on every page of your site. Avoid technical jargon and an overt sales pitch. Don't attempt to persuade your site visitors through unwanted and overbearing pressure. Provide effective information and they'll want to come back for more.

Key elements of your VPO should include:

- One click, a speedy download and journalists should be able to access all current and archived news releases. This means recent headlines with dates and a two-line story synopsis.
- An easily understandable symbol shows what is corporate, financial or product news, along with case studies, policy papers and surveys.
- The first sentence of each story briefly summarizes the main facts of the article.
- Each news release should be supported by up-to-date contact information including name, phone, e-mail, fax and address.
- Feature virtual press packs – a handy way for journalists to get all the information they need about a company in one quick,

convenient package. Compress files using a tool like Winzip or Stuffit to minimize download time.

- Include a link associated to relevant pictures and graphics. JPEG (.jpg) images are the standard format for image files – they compress well and require less download time.

- A quick look at the site should reveal small pictures (known as thumbs), which, when clicked on, enlarge for detail. Photos should also feature factual captions with a date and media copyright release details.

- News releases may include an internet link to expert or executive commentators where appropriate.

- Each new release should have a full search capability along with options to search the VPO, associated story links and the full website by keyword.

- Feature hyperlinks to real-time and sector-specific news at sites such as the BBC, CNN, AP, Reuters and PR Newswire to add credibility and a sense of context to your VPO.

- Allow for an opt-in capability for journalists to receive information from and about your business. Journalists can elect to receive short headers plus a URL link to stories as e-mail alerts, e-mails with text stories and an 'opt-in' choice of subject matter, such as corporate, financial, product launch or case study. The VPO can then welcome a journalist at the next visit with a personalized 'Hello, John. Welcome back. You may be especially interested in this story about...'

Follow these core guidelines and in no time visiting reporters will be able to take a story and add rich and up-to-date content, news, expert opinion from the organization and independent third-party facts and expertise. With so much valuable material available, journalists will most likely sign up for the VPO's e-mail newsletter and automatically updated new story function.

For all of this to work effectively it is important that the content for your VPO is fresh and up to date. A stale VPO reflects poorly on the company and will not encourage journalists to return regularly.

A well-constructed VPO should also include an internal 'content management system' that allows any authorized person to update and expand it without requiring web programming skills.

Remember, adding a VPO to your PR arsenal shouldn't require a complete website redesign. A VPO can be, in effect, a separate website, with a simple link from the home page, labelled along the lines of 'press office' or 'news'. It is important that the VPO's branding, look and feel closely match your main website. This will provide it with the appearance of being an authentic, official and definitive source of corporate information (see Figure 4.7).

An internet community

The world wide web is such an everyday feature of our lives that it seems hard to believe that it is barely 12 years old as of 2005 (e-mail and the internet came on the scene decades ago).

For PR practitioners the value of the web lies in its immense potential for quick, cheap and easy two-way communication. A good example of this is the online auction site eBay. The most successful non-search engine internet site today, eBay has developed beyond being just a shopping site and moved into the realms of a 'community'.

As eBay rapidly gained in popularity, its founder – Pierre Omidyar – realized he could not possibly hope to keep up with answering the growing number of buyers' and sellers' questions about how to use the site. Therefore, by including their e-mail addresses, Omidyar allowed users to communicate directly with each other, helping them to solve their own problems. In doing so he created a message board that meant eBay users were able to share information with like-minded users who formed an entire community. The more self-sufficient the users became, the fewer demands they put on his limited time.

The newness of the web and its communication potential also offer up a series of fresh challenges to the PR practitioner. Communication via this medium is easily facilitated – so how do you differentiate your messages to stand out from the crowd? How do you compete against the sheer volume of information available? How do you effectively target or direct key stakeholders to your site?

By making information about your service available on the web, you naturally increase the possibility of take-up by your customers. However, for your advice, service or product promotion to work it must be both trusted and credible. A good example of success in this respect is Amazon.com, which pioneered the concept of reader reviews for the books the site sells.

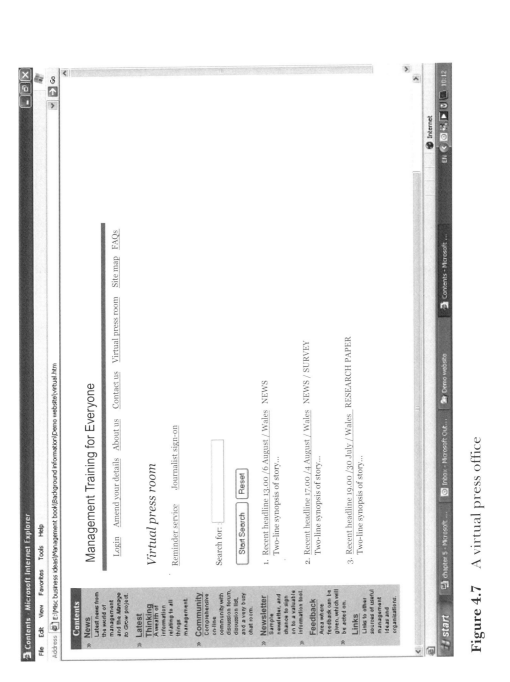

Figure 4.7 A virtual press office

When the web was conceived by Tim Berners-Lee, he envisaged it would be as easy to edit as it is to browse. Twelve years on, while the majority of people regularly browse, few create or edit their own web content.

However, this division between content creators and browsers is beginning to change. Firstly, many of the initially successful, design-rich websites failed following the stock market collapse of 2000. Secondly, the current trend for 'weblogging' by individuals is returning the web into the hands of the non-specialist.

To reach potential customers, while developing an 'online community' feel, it is important to consider building your site into a 'learning fountain'. This format will influence visitors by providing them with something new alongside information that helps them to learn. Such sites also offer an environment that allows visitors to submit and share their own articles. This process both adds credibility and encourages long-term repeat visits from people whose content is included on the site.

A website has the potential to reach a global audience, but it's more likely to appeal if it is differentiated by content that attracts visitors with a specific interest or connection.

In addition to being informed, people often visit specific websites to interact with other people. Filling this need will help you turn browsers into customers. Asking questions, raising issues, discussing problems – all of these steps will help develop an interactive community that breeds a form of brand loyalty.

PR practitioners are highly suited to this task as they are used to carefully focusing in on and choosing their target audiences, defining messages and selecting the best means to communicate them. Remember – it's not computers you want to communicate with; it's people.

Writing for the web means producing good, snappy copy that has impact and is easy to read, but there are also some crucial differences to consider between the printed word and writing for publication online. Key points to remember include:

- Write for skim reading. Don't assume a reader will begin at the beginning. Provide sub-headings as signposts and try to ensure that paragraphs make sense in isolation.
- Write for the screen rather than the page – break text into small, manageable chunks.

- Navigation and usability – make it easy for a reader to skip between pages and websites through appropriate use of hyperlinks.
- Write clearly and for a global audience – don't assume your readers will all be native English speakers.

Further to this, website content should be kept up to date – meaning a strong emphasis on news that is relevant to your target audience. Link your site to the outside world to provide credibility in the reader's mind. Also, provide internal links on every page: visitors may arrive at your site via your news release, so make it possible for them to jump from there to your home page or your contact details.

Discussion boards, forums and chatrooms will let your customers ask questions of you and each other. You should also solicit customer feedback and advice, giving visitors the impression that you care about their needs and are willing to make changes to your service if popular opinion suggests this is necessary.

In terms of what not to do with a website – don't be over-impressed by clever design or the use of Flash animations; avoid italics, over-the-top fonts, jargon and hype. Write clearly and objectively for an external audience.

Where to now?

If you are happy with all of the above, you are ready to start your PR campaign. Chapter 5 outlines how everything you have done up until now fits together, to give you the results that you've been hoping for.

5 Tactics

Introduction

This is where the tactics of the strategy come into play. We throw all sorts of suggestions at you, which you can easily implement as part of a successful PR campaign, such as developing research surveys; negotiating in-magazine surveys to be run in conjunction with leading publications; forming strategic alliances with appropriate partners to enforce the credibility and authority of a brand; increasing press coverage by drawing up media coverage targets; creating newsletters; getting celebrity endorsement; etc.

Recap

We have come a long way, but now we're nearing the final, crucial part of our PR journey. To see how everything fits together, go back through the book and reprise the following elements:

My business operates in a market that is _____, _____ and _____. My customers are _____, my suppliers are _____ and they see me as a _____ company.

The age of my customers is mostly _____ and their gender is mostly _____. As for their pockets, they are mostly _____. They are usually from _____ areas, and they mostly come out (in the) _____.

My business provides a _____, which I _____. It is a business that is _____ years old, and I am the _____ of it.

_____ got a mission statement written down, and _____ got the values of my business written down. _____ got business objectives that are written down, _____ got marketing and sales objectives that are written down and _____ got product-/service-specific objectives.

I am _____ of my product's or service's unique selling point(s), which I regard as _____ to my business.

_____ got a management structure in place, and there are _____ lines of reporting in place between different employees. I want the business to _____ over the next three to five years and, compared to my main competitor, I want to be _____.

PR has a _____ role in my business. _____ undertaken marketing and PR campaigns in the past. (If you *have*, fill in the rest of this paragraph). _____ is the way I would describe them, and _____ was the person in charge of the campaign(s).

I would characterize my firm and describe its main business focus as:

My suppliers, employees and customers perceive my business as (refer back to Chapter 1):

My strategic direction is (refer back to Chapter 1):

My overall PR objectives are (refer to Chapter 3):

Figure 5.1 shows what my stakeholder map looks like (refer to Chapter 4).

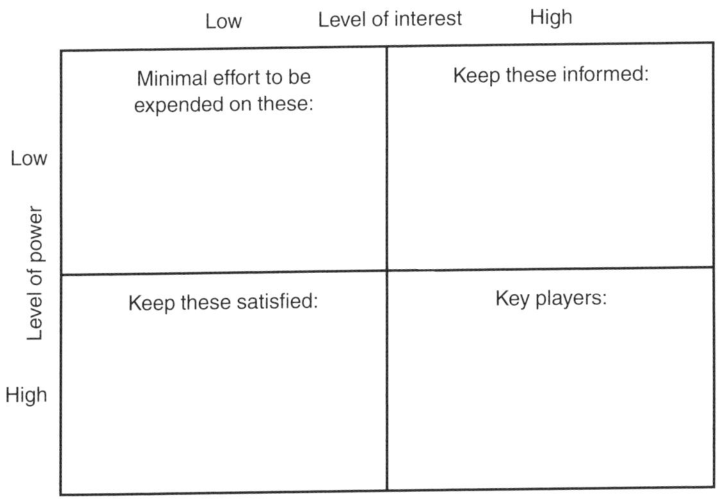

Low   Level of interest   High

	Low	High
Low (Level of power)	Minimal effort to be expended on these:	Keep these informed:
High	Keep these satisfied:	Key players:

Figure 5.1   Stakeholder map

Table 5.1 on the next page shows what my key stakeholders think and what I would like them to think.

I have the infrastructure in place to meet these objectives (refer to Chapter 1 and your audit):

☐ Yes   ☐ No

I have the website in place to meet these objectives (refer to Chapter 4):

☐ Yes   ☐ No

If you picked 'No' in either of the last two questions, you need to address these issues before continuing this process.

The next step

OK, now you're ready for the next step. You will need to keep referring to the last few pages, so it is important that you fill this previous section in. You now have an idea of where your business is in terms of

Table 5.1 What my key stakeholders think and should think

Priority	Stakeholder	Thinks now	Should think
1.			
2.			
3.			
4.			
5.			
6.			
7.			
8.			
9.			
10.			
11.			
12.			

PR; you have direction; you have objectives; you have a strategy to meet those objectives – now you need the tactics in order to finish the job!

Let's go back to Trevor's Terrific Travel Ltd. You may remember that their objectives were:

1. To market our high street stores so that 10,000 AB customers buy holidays from us by September 2006.
2. To continue to develop our IT infrastructure so that all our suppliers are communicated with by intranet by December 2006.
3. To develop our website so that 5,000 business customers use us by September 2006.
4. To develop our ICT systems so that we have a full in-house computerized training programme that trains 30 new recruits by July 2006.

Table 5.2 shows the types of messages they would use to communicate these objectives, and the channels through which they would send the messages.

Everything has a PR angle: basically, PR is about communicating effectively with different audiences. With this in mind, cast your mind back to Big Car Manufacturers plc who were planning to close down car production in one of their plants in Anytown, instead using the facility to research a new breed of diesel engines, but employing only a fraction of their current workforce. Their objectives would look something like this:

1. To position the plant as being at the forefront of developing the most efficient and environmentally friendly diesel engines on the market over the next 12 months.
2. To place the plant as being a model of employment practice over the next 12 months.
3. To give the plant an environmentally friendly image to complement its development of 'greener' engines over the next 12 months.

Table 5.3 shows what their comprehensive programme of PR tactics on the back of these objectives would look like.

Table 5.2 Trevor's Terrific Travel Ltd: communicating objectives

Mechanisms of change (measure no.)	Timescale	Percentage of budget
To market our high street stores so that 10,000 AB customers buy holidays from us by September 2006.		
1. Seeking coverage in as many publications as possible, both trade and media, about the new merger and its new customer focus.	Immediately	26
2. Develop some separate promotional material for the new venture, which should be distributed widely through the usual channels.	Begin planning immediately	10
3. Make sure the new website provides a good introduction to the new venture, ensuring that the necessary links are established and maintained.	Immediately	0
To continue to develop our IT infrastructure so that all our suppliers are communicated with by intranet by December 2006.		
4. To become active in lobby groups to push the issue of computerization of the tourism industry.	Immediately	2
5. To lead the debate in trade publications.	Immediately	2
6. To work in partnership with suppliers in order to promote the benefits of intranets and their successful implementation.	Immediately	5
To develop our website so that 5,000 business customers use us by September 2006.		
7. Develop a separate part of the site dedicated solely to business customers.	After 2 months	5
8. Fast-track business customers through the booking process and give them priority.	After 2 months	0
9. Heavily promote this aspect of the new company (though avoid specifically citing point 8 so as not to alienate other customers).	After 4 months	20
To develop our ICT systems so that we have a full in-house computerized training programme that trains 30 new recruits by July 2006.		
10. Create a new employee newsletter specifically informing them about these new developments, backed up by regular briefing sessions between management and union leaders to answer any questions and address concerns.	After 1 month	10
11. Advertise extensively in the trade press of this new development so as to attract bright new recruits.	After 2 months	20
12. Train existing staff so they will attract new recruits through word of mouth.	Immediately	0

Table 5.3 PR tactics for Big Car Manufacturers plc

Mechanisms of change (measure no.)	Timescale	Percentage of budget
Employees: to encourage employees to communicate effectively with management in order to improve relations.		
1. Create a new employee newsletter specifically informing them about these new developments, backed up by regular briefing sessions between management and union leaders to answer any questions and address concerns.	Within 6 months	1
2. Carry out a survey among all employees to get feedback about current working practices and how they want the plant to improve.	Immediately	5
3. Establish an official 'open-door' policy between senior management and any member of the plant's workforce to hear any work-related messages, concerns or suggestions.	Immediately	0
Consumers: to position the plant as the leading authority on new and improved diesel engines.		
4. To commission research on burning consumer issues regarding all motoring aspects, such as road safety issues, vehicle emission issues, motoring costs, etc, and to use this as the basis of the launch of new diesel engine developments at the plant.	Immediately	5
5. Establish information call centre detailing new products and where they can be purchased. Call centre to be extensively advertised and tied in with above tactic.	Immediately	37
6. To have a major presence at the British International Motor Show to distinguish the plant's position as a provider of new and exciting motor vehicle engine technology. A communications plan will be put in place to ensure that the plant's attendance at the event is clear to major audiences before, during and after the event. This will include an integrated approach using direct marketing, advertising and event tactics to encourage visitors to the plant's stand.	Begin planning immediately	7
Mainstream media: to use a range of techniques to ensure that key media feel that they are being properly informed, and that the plant's messages are being comprehensively explained and communicated.		
7. New techniques include going to the main media pools, such as the BBC's Wood Lane centre and ITN's Gray's Inn Road location, in order to promote the campaign's messages proactively. These visits will be followed by visits to journalists in their offices.	Immediately	0.5
8. A range of different backdrops will be prepared to ensure that photocalls receive maximum pick-up, and for different aspects of the campaign, ie new product development, employment practices and environmental concerns.	Immediately	1

Table 5.3 continued

Mechanisms of change (measure no.)	Timescale	Percentage of budget
9. A single database is to be prepared, connected to fax and e-mail engines to ensure speedy, efficient news and materials distribution.	Immediately	0.5
Technical and trade press: to generate interest in the new products that the plant will be developing.		
10. One of the target audiences at the British International Motor Show (see under 'Consumers').	Begin planning immediately	See 6
11. Key trade publications to be researched and features targeted to ensure that the plant's objectives are communicated.	Immediately	0.5
12. An advertising campaign to build awareness of the exciting new products that the plant will be working on.	Begin planning immediately	9
Politicians: to increase awareness of the plant's new employment policies.		
13. Use the employee survey as a basis to promote the changes that the plant will make to working practices and the new, more open employee communication policies.	Begin when survey results complete	0.5
14. Conduct interviews with targeted politicians to gain in-depth understanding of issues of importance surrounding employment practices at the plant.	Immediately	0.5
15. Create a section of Big Car Manufacturers plc's website dedicated specifically to the plant and the progress surrounding its new employment practices (including case studies), and make sure this is communicated to politicians.	Within 6 months	0.5
Shareholders: to recognize that not all shareholders are based in London.		
16. To schedule and produce roadshow presentations in Cardiff, Birmingham, Leeds, Glasgow and London specifically aimed at informing shareholders of the campaign objectives.	Within 6 months	9.5
17. An information pack to be written and supplied to shareholders, briefing them on the campaign and requesting their support.	Immediately	4
18. A 'virtual' launch of the new campaign, emphasizing the benefits of investing in an industry with a future. Viewers who log on at the time of the launch will be greeted with an exciting loading screen, followed by a short Flash video detailing the new mission of the plant.	Within 6 months	1
Banks: to get them to frame the plant as being at the cutting edge of new vehicle technology.		

Table 5.3 continued

Mechanisms of change (measure no.)	Timescale	Percentage of budget
19. To be included in the 'virtual' launch, as detailed above.	Within 6 months	See 18
20. To direct them to the key trade publications where features will be targeted to ensure communication of the plant's new direction.	As soon as features are published	0.5
21. To develop a newsletter to be sent out to bank managers highlighting new innovations, sourcing contributions from high-profile third parties such as Jeremy Clarkson, Alistair Darling MP, etc, in order to position the plant as industry experts.	Within 6 months	1
Environmental groups: to increase commitment to environmental roles and communicate this outside.		
22. Launch of an environmental challenge aimed at schools with prizes for those that undertake the small-scale creation or restoration of an area important for wildlife and the local community.	Within 6 months	2
23. To raise the profile of the plant's positive role in combating environmental issues through the news (print and broadcast) media, and to secure a page on Big Car Manufacturers plc's website for this element of the campaign.	Within 6 months (tie in with above)	0.5
24. To work with the local authority on its Local Agenda 21 Partnership, specifically addressing environmental aspects, such as its wildlife, waste, water and energy strategies.	Immediately	4
Dealers: to inform them of the plant's new direction, and help the plant in its media campaign.		
25. One of the target audiences at the British International Motor Show (see under 'Consumers').	Begin planning immediately	See 6
26. A dealer survey to be conducted to establish communication lines between themselves and the plant's PR agency and generate local media coverage.	Begin planning immediately	1
27. Communication links to include a newsletter, a dedicated dealer hotline to provide local PR support, and attendance at dealer association meetings to deliver briefings, update, provide support and generate stories about the plant's new products.	Within 6 months	5
Community leaders: to form a partnership by encouraging as many residents as possible to become involved with the regeneration process.		
28. Media awareness training for residents: to ensure local people are prepared to deal with the press and provide a positive image for the community.	Within 6 months	1

Table 5.3 continued

Mechanisms of change (measure no.)	Timescale	Percentage of budget
Employees: to encourage employees to communicate effectively with management in order to improve relations.		
29. Press announcements and conferences: announcements to the press being proactive instead of reactionary. Provide a positive image of the community.	Within 6 months (tie in with above)	0.5
30. To conduct a series of community-led events, providing platforms for access between the new partnership and the community.	Within 6 months (tie in with above)	1
Suppliers: to keep them informed about the health and future opportunities of the plant's work.		
31. One of the target audiences at the British International Motor Show (see under 'Consumers').	Begin planning immediately	See 6
32. To include them on the mailing list for the newsletter highlighting innovations, positioning the plant as industry experts.	Within 6 months	0.5
33. To direct them to the key trade publications where features will be targeted to ensure communication of the plant's new direction.	As soon as features are published	0.5
Other car manufacturers: to work together to ensure the health of the UK motor industry.		
34. To use the research on burning consumer issues regarding all motoring aspects, and to use this as the basis for a new partnership approach to ensuring the health of the motor industry.	Within 8 months	0
35. To become active in lobby groups, eg the Society of Motor Manufacturers and Traders Ltd (SMMT), to push these issues.	Immediately	0

Pretty comprehensive! Before launching into your own plan of action, there are a few tactics that you might want to consider, many of which are featured in Table 5.3:

- Communicating complex messages.
- Differentiating yourself from the competition.
- Positioning yourself as an authoritative industry voice, with an in-depth understanding of your particular market.
- Identifying audiences and an appropriate strategy in order to form an 'alliance of interests' with them.

- Balancing your media stance away from sensationalist to educational editorial.
- Getting PR to hold together a consistent message while at the same time targeting diverse audiences with tailored messages.
- Turbocharging your sales by creating awareness, excitement and demand for your products or services.
- Finding new ways to highlight 'must-buy' features, based on credible press and third-party content.
- Producing a three-stage strategy based on influential media penetration, independent advocacy and a comprehensive product review programme. It is designed to reach individual target groups with tailored messages and information on relevant, innovative product features using third-party 'champions' and industry partners to reinforce positive impressions and help convert awareness into sales.
- Undertaking crisis management: informing the context (explaining and promoting honest debate); keeping key people informed; avoiding finger pointing or diversionary blame tactics; moving the debate on.
- Repositioning your product or service as an aspirational one through tie-ins with other respected brands (forming strategic alliances with 'posh' companies).

Case study

The following case study shows that even big companies have to find new ways of pushing their brands.

Background

In 2001, a turning point for the IT industry in the UK was reached. Solid growth every quarter over the previous 10 years had made it the media and the City's darling. But cracks were starting to appear. Tough economic conditions, stagnating sales and missed quarterly forecasts by the industry big guns had dented its image. As a result, the whole industry was looking to the launch of Microsoft Windows XP to put down a marker for renewed growth and a brighter future. Could XP re-energize the industry and move IT back to the top of the business news agenda?

The launch of Windows XP was far from straightforward. Microsoft was attempting for the first time to sell a single operating system to multiple audiences: how could PR hold together a consistent and integrated campaign while targeting diverse audiences with tailored messages and helping Microsoft realize its and the industry's goals?

Objectives

August.One, the chosen PR agency, needed to create and implement a plan that satisfied two key aims:

1. *Turbocharge sales:* Microsoft had ambitious business and consumer sales targets for Windows XP. PR had to tie directly to these sales objectives based on easily measurable, targeted activities.
2. *Re-energize the PC market and create awareness, excitement and demand:* Windows XP was launching into an IT marketplace in recession. If it was to reach its sales targets, Microsoft needed to re-energize the market and the press and engage the wider IT industry.

Plan and strategy

Building awareness and driving sales in the face of an IT sector slowdown presented a unique challenge. As ever, maximizing positive press coverage was key, but the real challenge was in finding new ways to highlight 'must-buy' features for both a business and consumer audience – based on credible press and third-party comment. At the same time, engaging partners and competitors from across the IT industry would feed a groundswell of opinion and advocacy that would help reignite the IT marketplace.

August.One developed a three-stage strategy based on influential media penetration, independent advocacy and a comprehensive product review programme. It was designed to reach individual target groups with tailored messages and information on relevant, innovative product features using third-party 'champions' and industry partners to reinforce positive impressions and help convert awareness into sales.

Execution and implementation

*   Developing audience awareness depended on media relationships and understanding. The campaign kicked off with a comprehensive publishing house tour. The August.One team leveraged press contacts to organize meetings with all of the key publishing houses. This was a huge logistical task, but provided a solid foundation for the rest of the campaign. It initiated understanding of the product and established open press relationships from the word go. It offered press contacts the chance to see and use the product and provided a foundation from which to influence a vast readership.

- This enabled August.One to roll out one of the largest and most successful product review programmes ever seen in the UK. Established relationships with reviewers and personalized product previews ensured the desired focus on key product features and supported August.One's launch goals.
- A closely managed customer trial programme created a series of advocates with practical knowledge of the product. It provided opportunities for credible one-to-one interviews with influential press contacts and offered powerful third-party endorsement of the product.
- Competitions were launched in regional and specialist publications across the country, while a further press relations initiative drove media to events and conferences with an XP presence.
- Partner and industry press interviews, product placement and speaker programmes were critical to building critical mass and positioning XP as the IT industry's 'great white hope'. These initiatives were supported by pre-announcements and exclusives organized with close press contacts.
- The August.One team managed the entire partner and customer programme to ensure it delivered consistent, relevant and compelling PR content that supported Microsoft's dual objectives.

This array of activity culminated in a high-profile launch event, held at the Royal Festival Hall and attended by over 170 media representatives, Microsoft CEO Steve Ballmer, Microsoft partners and industry figures. Over 50 interviews were conducted with Microsoft and partners, while an exclusive interview with Steve Ballmer generated national, regional and online coverage across seven titles.

Results and evaluation

The campaign's objectives were achieved and in virtually every case exceeded:

- XP exceeded all sales targets: more than 7 million copies were sold in the first two weeks following launch (in comparison, Windows 2000 managed 3 million sales in its first four months).
- 80 per cent increase in home users likely to get Windows XP in the year following launch.
- 70 per cent increase in business users likely to get Windows XP in the year following launch.
- Overachieved on FY02 coverage target in Q1 alone: 441.5 million impressions (target: 400 million).
- Overachieved on Q1 print coverage: 98.5 million impressions (target: 80 million).
- Overachieved on Q1 online coverage: 321.3 million impressions (target: 100 million).

- Overachieved on publishing house tour: 30 publishing houses briefed (target: 11), which included 52 separate publications and an estimated 175–200 journalists.
- Overachieved on the press launch: 240 press registered, 170 attended (target: 105).

Tactics

So what sort of tactics can you employ? Here is a selection:

- Developing newsletters (we'll come to this later in the chapter): securing regular contributors from high-profile third parties.
- Developing research surveys: making them cost-effective by negotiating in-magazine surveys to be run in conjunction with leading publications.
- Forming strategic alliances with appropriate partners to enforce the credibility and authority of a brand (eg government bodies).
- Press coverage increase by drawing up media coverage targets, by using methods such as: approaching an appropriate medium on an 'exclusive' basis with advance briefings; acting as a hub press office during a campaign; writing national and regional press releases, and releases aimed at specialist press and online media.
- Commissioning fact sheets and informative guides to aid campaigns.
- Using freephone numbers for campaigns.
- Offering the press associated (but not expensive) gifts to provide 'creative standout'.
- Regional radio days to generate more in-depth interviews covering human interest angles.
- Securing early, heavyweight media endorsement, endorsement from analysts through face-to-face briefings, and recruitment of key media opinion informers.
- Opinion testing of opinion leaders, turned around quickly to inform and lead debate.
- Staged release of information to maintain awareness levels.
- Organization of roadshows.
- Rapidly rebutting attacks by competitors.
- Developing backdrops for photocalls.

- Developing a campaign database connected to fax and e-mail engines to ensure speedy, efficient news and materials distribution.
- Report commissioning of independent academics.
- Facilitating media awareness training for relevant people in the company, to ensure they are prepared to deal with the press and provide a positive image (again, dealt with below). Often company members are the most effective spokespeople for the company itself, as they are both passionate and knowledgeable about the area and their future plans.
- Approaching media about being assigned a contact to cover all subsequent stories emanating from a campaign, and support for creating a campaign identity by reproducing a logo alongside associated stories.
- A 'Whatever Week' involving hosting special events and promotions, incorporating posters, folders, leaflets and tentcards.
- Getting messages in soap opera storylines.
- Creating limited-edition media kits that are personalized for journalists.
- Agenda setting through columns in local newspapers.
- Negotiating features with newspapers, offering human interest stories and topical case studies.
- Launching viral campaigns to direct visitors to the relevant part of organizations' websites using a database of e-mails.
- Using promotional vouchers.
- Starting up a competition.
- Sponsoring an event.
- Using celebrities to aid product or service launches.
- When dealing with high-technology companies, emphasis on generating word-of-mouth endorsements, with early adopters being encouraged to talk up the company and product (in media, at conferences, etc).
- Publication of an e-zine to publicize customer news, with invitations to subscribe to it on websites.
- Using below-the-line marketing techniques (eg on the back of business account bank statements, etc).
- Attending business exhibitions.
- Holding stakeholder forums in unique venues with high-profile facilitators.
- Creating CD ROM 'media toolkits'.

- Creating a 'new contract' with stakeholders.
- Using a launch technique where journalists are sent a teaser that leads them to a page on a website. The idea is to maintain the secrecy of a bold claim while stimulating interest in the media. Once at the site the journalist discovers various video clips of people waiting for something, such as a clock ticking, someone waiting at traffic lights and a father waiting for the birth of a baby. There is also a counter to the launch day.

Website PR

It is very easy to get wrapped up in the intricacies of creating a website, but here we must remember that it is merely a means to an end – to help you realize your PR objectives. When you have taken the section on website design into consideration, you should have a credible website with which to take on the PR world. To use it effectively, you will have a publishing cycle for your target media. It should look something like this:

1. Go over your site with a fine-tooth comb, making sure the information on it and all its links are updated and refreshed. It needs to be completely accurate because, if there are any mistakes on it, the press will pick them out.
2. Create an 'online press pack': this should contain details of the key communications you are trying to get out into the wider world. Include items such as product information, company reports, a breakdown structure of your firm's operations and who is responsible for what, and your firm's location, phone and e-mail contact details. It should also contain high-resolution digital photos that you can give the press to use in print.
3. Next, you need to tap into your sales skills and call the press on the phone. The object here is to establish some rapport with them and get an idea of what sort of stories they might want from you.
4. The next thing is the hardest bit. You need to put together an actual story that journalists can use, which is aimed at their readers, and it has to be newsworthy. Fortunately, the section below gives you a few pointers.
5. At all costs, avoid sending out 'non-news'. This includes announcements of new staff, a new website or new customers.

6. Next, you need to get a press release out to the right people, so you should draft up a 'key media contacts' list in publications that you are trying to target.
7. The timing of your press release is all-important, to try to fit it in with the publication date of your targeted media. For example, if they go to print on a Thursday, send it out on the Wednesday morning.
8. When you have finished your press release, put it with your online press pack.

So what's newsworthy?

Here are a few ideas on the kind of stories that newspapers generally publish:

- *Create a benchmark.* Publish a weekly or monthly statistic, usually called a 'barometer', which tracks over time the behaviour of your customers.
- *Publish a rant.* Be controversial. Put together a paper that completely opposes conventional wisdom, which journalists can create drama with by drawing in other views to have a 'heated debate'.
- *Hold an event.* You can arrange a conference, either online or offline, which can have a very topical or controversial theme. With some heavyweight speakers and good advance notice to the press, you can generate two lots of coverage: the first will be the announcement of the event, and the second will be based on the event itself.
- *Present an award.* Consider cooperating with a trade body or recognized independent organization and either sponsoring or judging its award ceremonies.
- *Publish a report.* Link up with a university and get it to conduct a piece of research that is both useful to it and useful for your own PR purposes. If the report is topical enough, you're bound to get good coverage.

Website online evidence pack

Consider creating an 'online evidence pack'. This is essentially a series of 'private pages'. The idea here is that you gather together a range of successful case studies and other business ideas that you have 'in the pipeline'. You set up these addresses with your web hosters, but don't publish them anywhere on your site or on search engines. There is nothing particularly valuable about these pages, but they are hidden from the rest of the world. You should even remove the gloss from them and give them the appearance of materials for staff, maybe even password-protect them. Now you pass on the addresses – usually one or two only – in a discreet manner to your target journalists, who perceive they have 'inside information'. And they do! It's a great way to impress and get good PR.

Over to you...

There is obviously a whole wealth of ideas here, and you could get quite overawed by them all. The trick is to pick out the ones that are most relevant to you and your objectives, and the ones that you think you will have most success with. So, take a look back at the 'Recap' section at the beginning of this chapter and, with these fresh eyes, take a look at what Trevor's Terrific Travel Ltd and Big Car Manufacturers plc did; then look at all the other tactics on offer, including those mentioned in the case study. Having done this, take a deep breath and fill in Table 5.4.

It's good to have a raft of great ideas, but each one will come with a cost. And you're in business, right? So how much is this going to cost you? This is where we link your new strategy to a budget. Look at Table 5.4 and judge how much each measure is going to cost, phoning up for quotes if possible. Then enter your results in Table 5.5.

Now that you have an idea of costs, there really is nothing to stop you getting on with putting your strategy into operation. But wait! Before doing anything there are two main areas where most people who dabble in PR fall down: how to write a newsletter and how to handle the media. The remainder of this chapter will deal with these two issues.

How to write a newsletter

Internal and external newsletters, it has to be said, have never been the fastest forms of communication. But just as you wouldn't want to

Table 5.4 Reaching your objectives

How you will reach your objective (objective no.)	Timescale	Percentage of budget
Objective:		
1.		
2.		
3.		
Objective:		
4.		
5.		
6.		
Objective:		
7.		
8.		
9.		
Objective:		
10.		
11.		
12.		

read last week's newspaper, you shouldn't expect employees and customers to want to read old information in their newsletters.

External newsletters can be very effective for promoting a company's new products and services, maintaining client relationships and building your reputation with existing customers. By communicating periodically with both your potential and existing customer bases, you generate increased interest in your business and subsequently improve your chances of improving future sales.

Table 5.5 Linking your strategy to a budget

Measure no.	Cost
1.	£
2.	£
3.	£
4.	£
5.	£
6.	£
7.	£
8.	£
9.	£
10.	£
11.	£
12.	£
Total for 12 measures	£

However, before going any further, think carefully about your target readership. Is a newsletter the right format for your communication plans? For example, if you want a company's employees to be aware of key issues before they read about them in the press, a weekly or monthly newsletter is not going to work. It may, however, provide a useful environment for a considered summary of developments.

Understanding your audience is an important part of good newsletter production. This doesn't automatically necessitate regular, intensive reader surveys (although you may want to survey them from time to time). Newsletter production is a creative process as well as a business one, and you should aim to surprise readers by introducing something new to them in every edition.

Far too often newsletters are badly put together and so fail to inform credibly. Newsletter content should be newsworthy, and this means being both topical and timely. With this in mind there are a number of important things to consider when producing a company newsletter:

- Set objectives. What is the purpose of your newsletter? Is it to promote new products or services? Is it to enhance your reputation? Is it a product in its own right, providing customers with high-value information not available anywhere else on your website? Is it a sales support tool that will underpin offline sales and wider marketing activity? Once you settle on one or two of these you can divide the newsletter into sections, each one addressing a single objective.

- Choose a name that will grab readers' attention. Your company name plus 'news' sounds very much like a promotional puff. Readers have to make a connection with a business before they can register any sense of value in its newsletter. Try something that's imaginative, implies news and interest value, and suits the demographic profile of your targeted readership.

- Create a production schedule. Decide on the frequency of your newsletter: once a week, once a fortnight or once a month? This will in large part depend on your editorial resources and the requirements of your audience. Try to establish what your readers' expectations are by asking them directly. There's little point in drowning customers with news if they prefer an update every three months.

- Define your content. Try to relate newsletter content as closely as possible to your objectives. If the newsletter is essentially promotional, make sure you describe new products or services along with their prices, benefits and features. If the newsletter is essentially a reputation builder, be sure to publish recent case studies focusing on success stories and happy clients. If the newsletter is a product in its own right, make sure the content that you're publishing is original, provocative and what the audience expects.

- The design of your newsletter is best left to professional graphic designers. If the newsletter is of the e-mail variety, ensure that the vast majority of your customer base has high-speed access to the internet.

- Employ journalistic techniques. Newsletters must contain news, not just announcements. News, by definition, is new – all the rest is just advertising.

- Cut the corporate jargon – you want your newsletter to be read, so make it interesting. External audiences don't read jargon-laden corporate gobbledegook, and you shouldn't expect employees to wade through it either.

- Understand your audience – you are writing for the readership, not management. Communications sent don't equal communications received: just because your message is out there, it does not necessarily mean anyone will read or understand it. Talk in the language of your audience: neither up nor down, but appropriately.
- Vary the flow – length doesn't equate to importance, so mix the length of stories to provide variety. 'News in brief' columns can increase the number of topics covered and can be written quickly.
- Balance the tone by mixing business messages with stories about real people. For every serious item, include something that is more light-hearted.
- Choose an attractive format. What will your audience find the most palatable? Sixteen A4 pages or eight A3 pages? What's easiest for distribution? If you are publishing on the web, what constitutes a page? How many links can one story manage?
- Great publications develop over time, but you won't be able to make substantial design changes every time you publish. Get as much as you can right first time.
- A picture tells a thousand words – so use photos, cartoons and graphics to support stories. Invest in a digital camera and encourage employees to use it for pictures to illustrate their stories.
- 'What's in it for me?' This is an inevitable question relating to corporate announcements. A new business unit may mean a reorganization that can affect jobs. Does a profits warning foretell redundancies? Perhaps beating forecasts raises hopes of big pay rises? Make stories personal in a way that has relevance to your audience.
- It's often hard to start a lively letters page but, as with local and national newspapers, they are generally well read. Never be tempted to invent correspondence. If an employee submits a story that you don't think is quite strong enough for the news or features columns, suggest the employee pens a short letter instead.
- The best newsletters are edited, not just published. Editorship requires a philosophy. What exactly are you trying to achieve with your publication? Is it a tool for disseminating corporate information or an enjoyable read that engenders community?
- Finally, use appropriate language – as always, plain, simple English is best. Even in internal publications, use acronyms and jargon

sparingly. There's no guarantee everyone in the organization will be as acquainted with the terminology as the managers who sign off copy.

How to handle the media

If you're looking for an improved public profile and you're effective at what you do, then at some point you or your close colleagues will find themselves in front of the media. This is, of course, what you've been after all along. But now you have their attention it is important to review the detail of your messages while proceeding with the utmost caution – after all, there is still some debate raging about all publicity being good publicity.

Working in communications, there is no way round this. Prominent figures such as senior company executives, public officials and politicians cannot avoid facing the media at one time or another in today's 24-hour 'information age'. Whether you operate at local community level or in national affairs, at some time a microphone or camera will be thrust in front of you and you will be required to make a statement that will be read, heard or seen by thousands of people.

Before agreeing to a media interview, two important questions to ask yourself are 'Do I need to do it?' and 'What's in it for me?' Dependent upon the situation and before agreeing to take part, listen carefully to the request. Don't be flattered or pressured into an interview. Find out as much as you can. Most importantly, you need to consider what the interview will achieve for your organization.

Companies and individuals successful in dealing with the media usually have a policy of fast-tracking media inquiries and responding to media requests immediately. So steps you should consider to help progress media contact include:

- Brief reception to fast-track media calls. All callers should be identified and calls or messages from journalists should be passed immediately to a nominated person for quick response.
- Return all media calls immediately – even if it is to say that you need more time to obtain information. If you don't call back quickly, journalists under the pressure of deadlines will look for alternative sources. Let them know that you are chasing up some facts and will have them within a specified time – preferably before their deadline.

- Nominate appropriate spokespersons, preferably more than one. Invariably a principal spokesperson will be unavailable on some occasions through business commitments, holidays, overseas travel and so on.
- Provide after-hours contact numbers if possible. The media do not work nine to five Monday to Friday. Most media operate around the clock including at the weekend and on public holidays. The content of Monday morning newspapers has to be researched and compiled on Sundays. You and your organization will be at an advantage if you provide media with after-hours contact numbers.
- Train your media spokespersons in communication skills and the techniques of media interviews. You need to find coaching and advice from a proper media trainer.

The first thing that you have to remember is that the media are not monsters. The functions of the media in modern democracies such as those in the United States, Europe, Canada and Australia are best described under what is termed 'the social responsibility theory' of the media. The functions under this model are about:

1. servicing the political system by providing information, discussion and debate on public affairs;
2. enlightening the public so as to make it capable of self-government;
3. safeguarding the rights of the individual by serving as a watchdog against government;
4. servicing the economic system, primarily by bringing together the buyers and sellers of goods and services through the medium of advertising;
5. providing entertainment;
6. maintaining their own financial self-sufficiency so as to be free from the pressures of special interests.

The 'devil's advocate' role pursued by the media is one of the reasons that negative stories make news more than positive stories. Journalists argue that the public is targeted with advertising, propaganda and public relations campaigns through a range of channels. They see it as their job to provide a balance. That means focusing on the bad news: the failure more than success; the breakdown rather than smooth operation; the accident rather than safety; the crime rather than virtue; the evil rather than good.

Journalists and editors contend that your company or organization will already be boasting about its successes, proclaiming its product virtues and noting its safety standards through advertising, public relations, promotions, direct marketing and other corporate communications. However, it does not preclude good news – or at least balanced news.

If you examine news stories, you will find that news is:

- dramatic;
- topical;
- specific with details, especially numbers; and
- relevant to the media's audiences.

You also need to remember that news is competitive. Editors and news directors report that, for every story published and broadcast, at least another 10 are discarded. In some major national and city media, as few as one in a hundred available stories are selected. Your news and comments have to compete to 'get a run' at the expense of other material. You can increase the competitiveness of your information by ensuring your statements to the media contain as many of the above criteria as possible. Your news and statements may not involve conflict or drama – indeed, you may not want them to – but you should try to score at least three out of four to be newsworthy.

When it comes to your interview, you need to consider all the possible options. For example, if the interview is for TV and will take place at your premises, consider backdrops that prominently feature your logo. Also, think about whether you want to be interviewed in an area that is bustling with people (to perhaps demonstrate the vibrancy of a firm) or whether you would prefer a quieter location (to imply calm and sobriety).

As an interviewee, you are entitled to some basic information, including

- What station and programme is your interviewer from?
- What sort of programme is it?
- When is it going out?
- Who watches it?
- Who else is taking part and what views do they hold?

- What question areas do they want to discuss?
- Who with and how long?
- Is it live or pre-recorded?

While this may seem like a fairly extensive checklist to consider, just relax – if you can recall nothing else when it comes to the crunch, just remember that the key to a good interview is largely down to good preparation.

The interview itself is no time for original thought – the last thing you want is to be caught out by a question that startles you. The best interviews are carefully planned and rehearsed. Think about this when considering a candidate for the role of spokesperson. Research shows that, as with any good presentation, content accounts for just 7 per cent. The impact is in the voice (38 per cent) and, for TV, the looks (55 per cent).

Company spokespeople often naively face media interviews ill equipped for the dynamic communication opportunity that media interviews provide. Some basic tips and training can equip you to get your points across in an interview and minimize misreporting and misquoting.

Your first rule of thumb is to develop two or three key messages. Then:

- Prepare a Q&A sheet. Brainstorm any nasty Qs.
- Assess the reaction of the target audience.
- Select lively examples to buttress your case.
- Arm yourself with several fascinating facts or statistics about your business.
- Practise by doing a dry run.
- Don't 'learn' the Q&A sheet, as this will make you sound too scripted.

Journalists are trained to ask probing and sometimes difficult questions. When you talk to the media, your company's reputation, the sales of your product or service, and your success or failure could depend on how you perform and how the interview turns out. Most interviews will result in only a short 'grab' of around 30 seconds or less of what you say.

A leading radio or TV show can expose your company or organization and your products or services to an audience of thousands or even millions. Similarly, major circulation newspapers and magazines reach large segments of your market or stakeholders. Potential viewers, listeners or readers may include government officials, regulatory bodies, environmentalists, consumer organizations, your own staff and your competitors.

A successful interview is about achieving your objectives. You don't just want the journalist to go away happy with a story: you want to get your message across and present your point of view.

There are three principal reasons why interviews fail in terms of communicating what an interviewee wants to say:

- attitude;
- an imbalance of knowledge;
- lack of preparation.

This being the case, consider the following useful tips for media interview handling skills. Before the interview or at the studio most people panic and forget everything they are meant to say, so:

- Arrive early.
- Keep distractions and stress low.
- Take a colleague.
- Check out any last-minute changes to the item.
- Avoid alcohol.
- Think about clothing, appearance and make-up.
- (If possible) meet the interviewer beforehand.
- Say nothing 'off the record'.
- Treat all cameras and mikes as being on.

With TV interviews, time is the one thing you don't have in an interview, as illustrated by the following equation of 'RelaTVty':

$$\text{Time divided by number of contributors divided by 2}$$
$$= \text{Your on-air contribution}$$

Divide by 2 to allow for the interviewer's introduction, questions and summary. So if you are invited to a four-minute live debate with three others, you'll have about 30 seconds to communicate your key points.

There are a number of interview styles. Most common is the prerecorded 'news'-style interview on location. This will be snipped into a couple of 10-second 'sound bites'. 'Remote' interviews, with you alone in a studio somewhere else, are also widely used. They are often live and rarely more than 90–120 seconds long. For this scenario, focus your eyes on the camera lens and pretend it's a person. Look interested throughout. React, nod and shake your head just as you would in a normal interview.

Radio is different. Radio is a one-to-one conversation with a listener at home or in a car. With no pictures, all the listener can judge you by is your voice. The three usual radio interviews are: in a studio, by telephone line; or via a reporter with a tape recorder. Make sure you can hear the presenter.

A phone-in means speaking live to your key audience. You may have more airtime than usual, but it can be fraught with danger, especially if you are asked questions for which you are unprepared. Maybe a caller has a genuine grievance. You can always suggest a point is followed up after the show.

Once seated for an interview you may be asked a random question for a 'sound-level check'. If you can, ask the interviewer what the first question is likely to be. Then:

- Maintain a conversational style.
- Avoid a quarrel. Attack the issue, not the interviewer.
- Get your main point in early.
- Stick to your planned agenda.
- Look the interviewer in the eye.
- Put everything into context.
- Don't use notes (on TV).
- Smile but beware of jokes.
- Be sympathetic, enthusiastic and brief.
- Don't ever, ever, walk out.

When it comes to interviews with the print media, and before you overreact to a negative story in the press, consider the following formula for newspaper impact:

- On average, only 10 per cent of a newspaper's circulation will read any one particular story in the paper. Some don't read the paper at all on some days and most people skip-read, selecting items of interest.
- On average, of those who read a particular story, most will remember only 10 per cent of the content.

This means that an average article in a newspaper with a circulation of 100,000 will only be read by 10,000 people and only 1,000 will remember what they read.

There is also research that shows that, even when awareness is created, attitudes do not necessarily change and, furthermore, when attitude change occurs it does not necessarily lead to behavioural change. So, even if 1,000 people remember what they read in the newspaper, only a small percentage of these will change their attitude because of the information and even fewer will change their buying behaviour.

When the media do come through to you, there are certain things you have to bear in mind. The oft-quoted KISS formula, or 'Keep It Simple Stupid', is critical in media interviews. You need to remember that, even if your topic is complex, the media's job is to explain it to a mass audience. Technobabble and professional mumbo-jumbo such as legalese will not be used by the media except in the specialist technical columns of trade journals.

Many interviewees believe it is friendly and a sign of their status or familiarity with the journalist to address an interviewer by name. They respond: 'Yes, John, the answer to that is…' or 'No, Jane, our company is not polluting the river.' You are not talking to the interviewer during interviews; you are talking to the audience, who may not see or even hear the interviewer. The interviewer is really only a conduit to the audience.

There are three other vital ingredients of all media interviews – honesty, sincerity and compassion or empathy. You should always be honest with the media. That does not mean that you have to tell journalists everything. But you should tell the truth in what you do say. Also, you should not be evasive in answering questions.

Avoid sarcastic responses such as 'As I already told you…' in answering repeated questions. The journalist is simply doing his or her job. Don't be affronted by journalists' assumption that you may be lying. Unfortunately, journalists are lied to every day. It is part of a journalist's job to play the role of the 'devil's advocate'. If you play it straight with journalists, most will soon recognize your honesty and relax their cynicism.

Don't be afraid to say you don't know. There will be times when you don't have the answer. Under no circumstances should you try to bluff your way through with the media. Just be honest and say, 'I don't know.' If the information is important to the story, offer to find out and get back to the journalist as quickly as possible.

Enthusiasm is a common by-product of sincerity. If you really believe in something, you become enthusiastic about it – and enthusiasm is a positive element in interviews. Enthusiasm is contagious. If you are enthusiastic, even cynical journalists will be at least a little affected by your energy and belief. And enthusiasm is often catching for the audience. Your enthusiasm should not be 'over the top'. Gushing propaganda and hype are not welcomed by the news media. But you don't have to be wooden either. When you have genuine enthusiasm or even passion for your subject, don't be afraid to let it show.

When you incorporate these basic ingredients into your media interviews – being readily accessible, speaking briefly, using simple language that ordinary people can understand and displaying honesty, sincerity and enthusiasm – you become recognized by the media as 'good talent'. 'Talent' is a trade term that the media, particularly radio and television, use for all interviewees and commentators. Journalists gravitate towards 'talent' whom they know can perform, so your ambition should be to earn their recognition as good talent, as this will open up many interview opportunities for you and your company.

6 The end has no end

Introduction

This is a summary chapter encouraging you to stick with your PR campaign and aiming to open up new avenues for your PR activities such as monitoring and evaluation; giving guidelines for selecting and briefing a media evaluation company; and setting out what to look for when working with a PR agency.

The end has no end

Welcome to the end! But, as they say, PR is a process, not an event. It is an ongoing process, and the more results it yields, the further you will probably want to delve into it. So how do you know what results you will have achieved? This is where the following section comes in...

Monitoring and evaluation

It is useful to consider monitoring and evaluation as forms of control: a means by which we ensure that objectives are achieved. We should constantly monitor the achievement of our objectives through a variety of ways, including involvement and observation, regular reporting, questioning and discussion, and records and routine statistics.

Let's go back to Trevor's Terrific Travel Ltd and its PR plan, shown in Table 6.1.

Table 6.1 PR plan of Trevor's Terrific Travel Ltd

Mechanisms of change (measure no.)	Timescale	Percentage of budget
To market our high street stores so that 10,000 AB customers buy holidays from us by September 2006.		
1. Seeking coverage in as many publications as possible, both trade and media, about the new merger and its new customer focus.	Immediately	26
2. Develop some separate promotional material for the new venture, which should be distributed widely through the usual channels.	Begin planning immediately	10
3. Make sure the new website provides a good introduction to the new venture, ensuring that the necessary links are established and maintained.	Immediately	0
To continue to develop our IT infrastructure so that all our suppliers are communicated with by intranet by December 2006.		
4. To become active in lobby groups to push the issue of computerization of the tourism industry.	Immediately	2
5. To lead the debate in trade publications.	Immediately	2
6. To work in partnership with suppliers in order to promote the benefits of intranets and their successful implementation.	Immediately	5
To develop our website so that 5,000 business customers use us by September 2006.		
7. Develop a separate part of the site dedicated solely to business customers.	After 2 months	5
8. Fast-track business customers through the booking process and give them priority.	After 2 months	0
9. Heavily promote this aspect of the new company (though avoid specifically citing point 8 so as not to alienate other customers).	After 4 months	20
To develop our ICT systems so that we have a full in-house computerized training programme that trains 30 new recruits by July 2006.		
10. Create a new employee newsletter specifically informing them about these new developments, backed up by regular briefing sessions between management and union leaders to answer any questions and address concerns.	After 1 month	10
11. Advertise extensively in the trade press of this new development so as to attract bright new recruits.	After 2 months	20
12. Train existing staff so they will attract new recruits through word of mouth.	Immediately	0

Table 6.2 shows the way in which they would control and monitor it.

Table 6.2 Controlling and monitoring the PR plan

Measure no.	Measurement	Timing
1.	Constant media monitoring to ensure accurate, comprehensive reporting of the total picture.	Ongoing
2.	Conduct independent report to gauge whether actions had significant impact on raising market awareness.	After 6 months
3.	Record number of 'hits' this part of website receives.	After 6 months
4.	Request a suppliers' meeting addressing these issues.	After 8 months
5.	Monitor clippings across trade press.	After 6 months
6.	Conduct survey to find out how many suppliers believe that the company has the right ICT strategy to take the industry forward.	After 8 months
7.	Record number of 'hits' this part of website receives.	After 6 months
8.	Internal records, part of everyday process.	After 6 months
9.	Conduct independent report to gauge whether actions had significant impact on raising market awareness.	After 6 months
10.	Feedback via employee focus groups.	After 6 months
11.	Monitor clippings across trade press.	After 6 months
12.	Conduct independent report to gauge whether training programme is successful.	After 6 months

Similarly, refer back to Chapter 5 and the monster PR plan of Big Car Manufacturers plc who were trying to turn their fortunes around. Table 6.3 shows an action plan of monitoring and evaluation measures.

Table 6.3 Action plan of monitoring and evaluation measures

Audience	Measure no.	Measurement	Timing
Employees	1.	Feedback via employee focus groups.	After 12 months
	2.	Reapply survey and compare results with original survey.	After 12 months
	3.	Feedback via employee focus groups.	After 12 months
Consumers	4.	Conduct independent report to gauge whether actions had significant impact on raising market awareness.	After 12 months
	5.	Record number and nature of calls to the information centre.	Review after 12 months
	6.	Obtain feedback via a comprehensive data list collated at the show by obtaining details of interested parties.	Immediately following motor show
Mainstream media	7.	Constant media monitoring to ensure accurate, comprehensive reporting of the total picture.	Ongoing
	8.	Record number of editorial inquiry responses.	After 12 months
	9.	Monitor clippings across the online, national, international and regional press.	Ongoing
Technical and trade press	10.	Monitor clippings across the technical and trade press.	Ongoing
	11.	Monitor and then evaluate numbers and nature of trade inquiries.	After 12 months
	12.	Record number of editorial inquiry responses.	After 12 months
Politicians	13.	Contact with Minister's offices for informal feedback.	After 12 months
	14.	Evaluate whether politicians' concerns are being met.	After 6 months
	15.	Record number of 'hits' this part of website receives and try to confirm if politicians have been using it.	After 12 months
Shareholders	16.	Conduct survey to find out how many shareholders believe that the plant has the right strategy to take the company forward.	Immediately after roadshows
	17.	With each information pack, a letter asking for feedback to be included, with responses to be compiled.	Immediately
	18.	Record number of 'hits' website receives on launch day and try to confirm if shareholders have been using it.	Immediately after launch

Table 6.3 continued

Audience	Measure no.	Measurement	Timing
Banks	19.	Record number of 'hits' website receives on launch day and try to confirm if banks have been using it.	Immediately after launch
	20.	A brand tracking survey to see if respondents make a strong or slight association between the plant and being an industry authority.	After 12 months
	21.	Feedback via audience focus groups.	After 12 months
Environmental groups	22.	Record how many children participated in the scheme.	Immediately after scheme ends
	23.	Monitor clippings across the online, national, international and regional press, and number of 'hits' on website.	Ongoing
	24.	Feedback from local authority in form of focus group.	After 12 months
Dealers	25.	Obtain feedback via a comprehensive data list collated at the show by obtaining details of interested parties.	Immediately following motor show
	26.	Record local media coverage and level of dealer involvement.	After 12 months
	27.	Questionnaire feedback on newsletter, number of dealer hotline calls to be recorded, dealer focus group established to gauge relationship.	After 12 months
Community leaders	28.	Constant media monitoring to ensure accurate, comprehensive reporting of community and plant's involvement.	Ongoing
	29.	Feedback via audience focus groups.	Ongoing
	30.	A post-event questionnaire to be sent to participants regarding the organization of the events and their understanding of the messages.	Immediately after events
Suppliers	31.	Obtain feedback via a comprehensive data list collated at the show by obtaining details of interested parties.	Immediately following motor show
	32.	A brand tracking survey to see if respondents make a strong or slight association between the plant and being an industry authority.	After 12 months
	33.	Obtain feedback via a series of meetings.	After 6 months
Other car manufacturers	34.	To request a manufacturer's meeting addressing these issues.	After 6 months
	35.	To evaluate SMMT progress in this area.	After 6 months

Now, of course, it's your turn. Using the above examples, list in Table 6.4 ways that you would monitor your own plan.

Table 6.4 Monitoring the plan

Measure no.	Measurement	Timing
1.		
2.		
3.		
4.		
5.		
6.		
7.		
8.		
9.		
10.		
11.		
12.		

As with most things, these measures will undoubtedly come with some costs attached. Fill in Table 6.5, judging how much each measure might be.

Table 6.5 Costs of the measures

Measure no.	Cost
1.	£
2.	£
3.	£
4.	£
5.	£
6.	£
7.	£
8.	£
9.	£
10.	£
11.	£
12.	£
Total for 12 measures	£

Media evaluation

When you undertake your PR campaign, it is essential that you know how your customers and stakeholders perceive your company. In the case of the media, it is difficult, as news pours out through newspapers, trade press, newsletters, broadcasting companies and the web.

It is often difficult to turn this wealth of disparate information into hard collated facts. But media evaluation provides vital knowledge about your competitors and markets, enabling you to tailor and adapt your PR campaign and measure the return on your investment.

You need to know:

- the media profile of your company;
- strengths and weaknesses and trends in your media coverage;
- how effectively your key audiences are being targeted;
- which messages are being received and, importantly, which are not;
- the perception of competitors' reputations, products and services;
- how much media space and audience reach your campaigns are achieving.

At this point, you may need to think about employing the services of a media evaluation company. This need not be expensive, and you should just take their basic package to see whether it's worth doing first. Such companies can be found through the Chartered Institute of Public Relations website (www.cipr.co.uk).

If you do decide to go down this road (which is much more recommended than trying to do it yourself), then you should ensure that your media evaluation company is properly briefed. You should therefore focus on the following:

- *Aims and objectives of your PR:* What are the criteria by which success will be judged and how will this information be used? The evaluation firm will help define objectives and design evaluation to complement other research.
- *What audiences you need to reach:* Selecting the right print, broadcast or other media, such as the internet, is critical in targeting either a tightly defined target group or a wider universe.
- *Where you are starting from:* Are there existing benchmarks from previous media measurement, perceptions on the organization or its competitors, or issues that might impact on PR? Show them your audit.
- *What key messages you want to track:* If possible, list them by audience. The media evaluation firm can help determine what is 'favourable' or 'unfavourable' and whether messages are actually measurable.
- *Which media are most relevant:* Getting in the 'nationals' is not the ultimate mark of success – it may be positively unhelpful, particularly if the story did not turn out as expected. Examine the objectives, messages and audiences to determine which categories of media are most relevant – regional, national, press, broadcast, the

internet, or an exclusive to achieve greater target accuracy and influence over content.

- *What scale of coverage you need:* In which regions of the UK or which countries? What media and languages? Cost is influenced by volume of items analysed and whether benchmark comparisons are involved.
- *What form of analysis you need:* The media evaluation firm will need to know format, frequency, degree of accuracy and who will use the information internally.
- *What the budget is:* An outside specialist may appear more 'expensive', but decide whether you have the time, skills and resources to do the job and what 'price' you would put on objectivity.

Factors in choosing a supplier should include the following:

- *What is their experience of similar jobs?* Take up references.
- *What form of analysis do they use?* Does this match your needs? Make sure you understand their definitions and terminology.
- *Who does the research?* Test their business understanding and the personal chemistry – the 'right' person should feel like a team member, not a supplier.
- *What structure and media?* Take advantage of the free consultancy that many firms will offer at the proposal stage.
- *How are findings presented?* Do you need just a management summary or the detail? Ask to see a sample presentation.
- *Other services?* Can they provide other services such getting feedback through interviews, surveys, focus groups and case studies, or offering additional media consultancy?

If you are insistent on doing it yourself or you want to put a 'toe in the water', then you might want to try Mass MediAudit®, which is a suite of planning and evaluation research tools for PR to use on Windows on a PC (www.masscom.com.au).

Working with a PR agency

In all of the case studies you have read in this book, you will have noticed that they have involved PR agencies. This is because, as successful as you might be in carrying out your campaign, nobody does it quite like the professionals. The purpose of this book has been to lay the groundwork for a campaign and to show you how valuable it can be. Should you have considerable success – and there is no reason why you shouldn't – then there will probably come a point where you can no longer focus on PR and have to focus on the successful business that it has created! Of course, if your PR efforts fall away, then so too will your business – it's a vicious circle!

It is then that you should look to employing the skills a PR agency offers. When you retain a public relations firm to help present your business to the public, you're forming an important strategic alliance. How much you get in return will depend on how much you put into the relationship.

Making the most of the services and expertise your public relations agency offers isn't difficult, but you have to put forth the effort from the beginning. When you do, you'll build a productive and successful partnership that should produce positive press and, eventually, increased revenue. There are three main ways to increase your chances of creating a successful and productive partnership with a PR agency:

1. *Nurture the relationship.* Be ready to spend a lot of time and effort up front to build the alliance. No matter how good your PR agency is, you'll have to inform your account representative about your company and industry. Ideally, you want your PR agency to know as much as you know about your business and the market it serves. The more time you spend getting them up to speed, the faster they'll be able to represent your company effectively.
2. *Keep them informed.* If your business is growing rapidly, you're probably taking on employees, opening accounts and releasing products at a dizzying rate. All these events represent outstanding opportunities for positive press, but your PR agency needs to know about them as early as possible. Open channels of communication between your business and the agency are critical. There's no magic rule about what works best – you can schedule weekly or monthly meetings with your PR firm or send all important memos to your account representative immediately. But it's essential to create a system to keep the agency informed and stick to it.
3. *Be an active listener.* Remember, you're the expert on your company, your customers and the products and services you offer. Your PR agency is the expert on crafting and delivering messages that will

present your business to the market in a positive and creative way. Don't underestimate the importance of active listening on both sides. You need to leverage each other's expertise to achieve the common goal of promoting your company.

Keep it going

I could give an uplifting motivational diatribe at this point, extolling the virtues of 'keeping going' and 'never giving up'. But instead, I'm going to leave this job to the President of the Chartered Institute of Public Relations, Chris Genasi:

I hope that through this book you've seen exactly how valuable public relations is. Whether you are looking at database marketing, guerrilla marketing, one-on-one marketing or whatever, PR is at the heart of everything you do. It's all to support selling through multiple channels, which in turn uses more technology options such as the internet or e-mail, which affects all your business planning and implementation. PR will focus your efforts into developing communications strategies that will build your business by really reaching your customers.

Your company's success hinges on more than market share. So you need to seek to reach all who are interested in your company: employees and communities, media, the government, investors and so on – you get the idea. You need to talk to everyone who wants to hear about you and what you do. And you must make sure that your messages present a consistent message about you.

Each customer is different. Their needs and expectations are as individual as you are. You need to work closely with them to learn those needs and expectations, and to develop the kind of communications programme you – and they – want. This is what PR is really about: understanding your key stakeholders and getting them to understand you.

Regardless of the size of your business, or the type of industry it operates in, communications are at the heart of delivering results and winning support. They are a critical force in business success because they have the power to affirm or change people's perceptions and behaviour. Because of their impact, communications can help or hinder a company's profitability, growth and market share. Communications are so important that they need to be strategically managed, just in the same way that operations, finance, administration, technology, human resources and other facets of your business are managed.

There has never been a time when effective communications have been more important. We have entered a business era that has been transformed by constant change and transition, leadership challenges, evolving technologies, and global markets that can best be described as unpredictable, lightning fast and unforgiving.

We are also witnessing the emergence of key stakeholder groups whose voices are resounding as strongly as those of members of the media, the financial community, industry analysts, the general public, customers, shareholders and employees. These groups – government regulators, special interest groups, policymakers, activists, ratings agencies, lobbyists and online and offline influencers – represent society's changing values. It is essential that today's businesses understand these new values; more closely align their behaviour with them; and create relevant, credible and transparent communications that satisfy the needs of their stakeholders.

Here's the obvious core of this approach: persuade your most important outside audiences with the greatest impacts on your business to your way of thinking. Then move them to take actions that help your business succeed.

The right action plan helps you to achieve that kind of success, and if you've put effort into following this book then the right action plan is what you should have. It will work by getting everyone working towards the same external audience behaviours. For example, people act on their own perception of the facts before them, which leads to predictable behaviours about which something can be done. When we create, change or reinforce that opinion by reaching, persuading and moving them to our desired actions, then the very people whose behaviours affect your business the most will be your greatest supporters – your public relations mission will be accomplished!

And look at what might happen: a nice jump in showroom traffic; local 'thought leaders' seeking your opinion on key local issues; newly interested prospects calling you; growing numbers of membership applications; the repeat purchase rate increasing; new inquiries about strategic alliances and joint ventures; capital givers making inquiries; and even politicians and legislators viewing you as a leading figure in the business community.

But you must really believe – deep down – why it's *so* important to know how your most important outside audiences perceive your operations, products or services. You must accept the reality that *perceptions* almost always lead to behaviours that can help or hurt your business.

Once you understand this, you are ready to do something about it. And the best way to do something about it is to go through this book and take seriously the exercises within it and carry them through. Then you will be ready for true PR success, which will put you head and shoulders above your competition.

It was Thomas Edison who said: 'Many of life's failures are people who did not realize how close they were to success when they gave up.' Don't fall into this category: the difference between perseverance and obstinacy is that one often comes from a strong will and the other from a strong won't. You need to embrace all the ideas in this book and see the many places they will take you. But for now I'll leave you with the salient words of the 30th President of the United States, Calvin Coolidge: 'Nothing in the world can take the place of persistence. Talent will not; nothing is more common than unsuccessful men with talent. Genius will not; unrewarded genius is almost a proverb. Education will not; the world is full of educated derelicts. Persistence and determination alone are omnipotent.'

Appendix

Help available for small businesses

The Business Link site (www.businesslink.gov.uk) provides easy access to practical and objective information and support for small businesses. In Scotland this service is Business Gateway (www.bgateway.com), in Wales it is (www.businesseye.org.uk), and in Northern Ireland it is (www.investni.com).

The DTI provides a small suite of grants, loans guarantees and subsidized consultancy to address a range of business issues – visit www.dti.gov.uk/bss

Young people wanting to set up a business can find advice and sometimes finance from the Prince's Trust (www.princes-trust.org.uk) and Livewire, which is sponsored by Shell UK Ltd (www.shell-livewire.org).

Most banks have arrangements to help customers in new and small businesses. You can also get business advice from professional accountants, solicitors and independent financial advisers.

The Chartered Institute of Public Relations offers access to PR information, advice and support, and provides training opportunities through a wide variety of events, conferences and workshops. You can find them at www.cipr.co.uk

The FSB is the largest campaigning pressure group promoting and protecting the interests of the self-employed and owners of small firms. It offers assistance and support to members and applies pressure on MPs, government and Whitehall. For more information, visit www.fsb.org.uk

MASS COMaudit® is a comprehensive suite of easy-to-use tools for low-cost, do-it-yourself planning and evaluation research of PR and corporate communication. Go to www.masscom.com.au

Smallbiz is a portal site to other websites that are useful to small businesses and entrepreneurs. The site is quick and easy to use and covers just about every aspect of running a small business, and can be found at www.smallbiz.uk.com

AdBriefing is a gratis website which is designed to help small business make more of their advertising and marketing efforts. The purpose of AdBriefing is to provide you with a monthly helping of copywriting tips and tutorials, written by people who supply a constant stream of ideas to make your promotional projects more powerful. Go to www.adbriefing.com

PR Week is a magazine which carries news and features about the public relations industry, and the online version can be found at www.prweek.com

PR Newswire is a news and press release distribution services for small business marketing, corporate public relations and investor relations, government and other organisations. Using *PR Newswire* you can reach a variety of critical audiences including the news media, the investment community, government decision makers, and the general public.

Index

NB: page numbers in *italic* indicate figures or tables